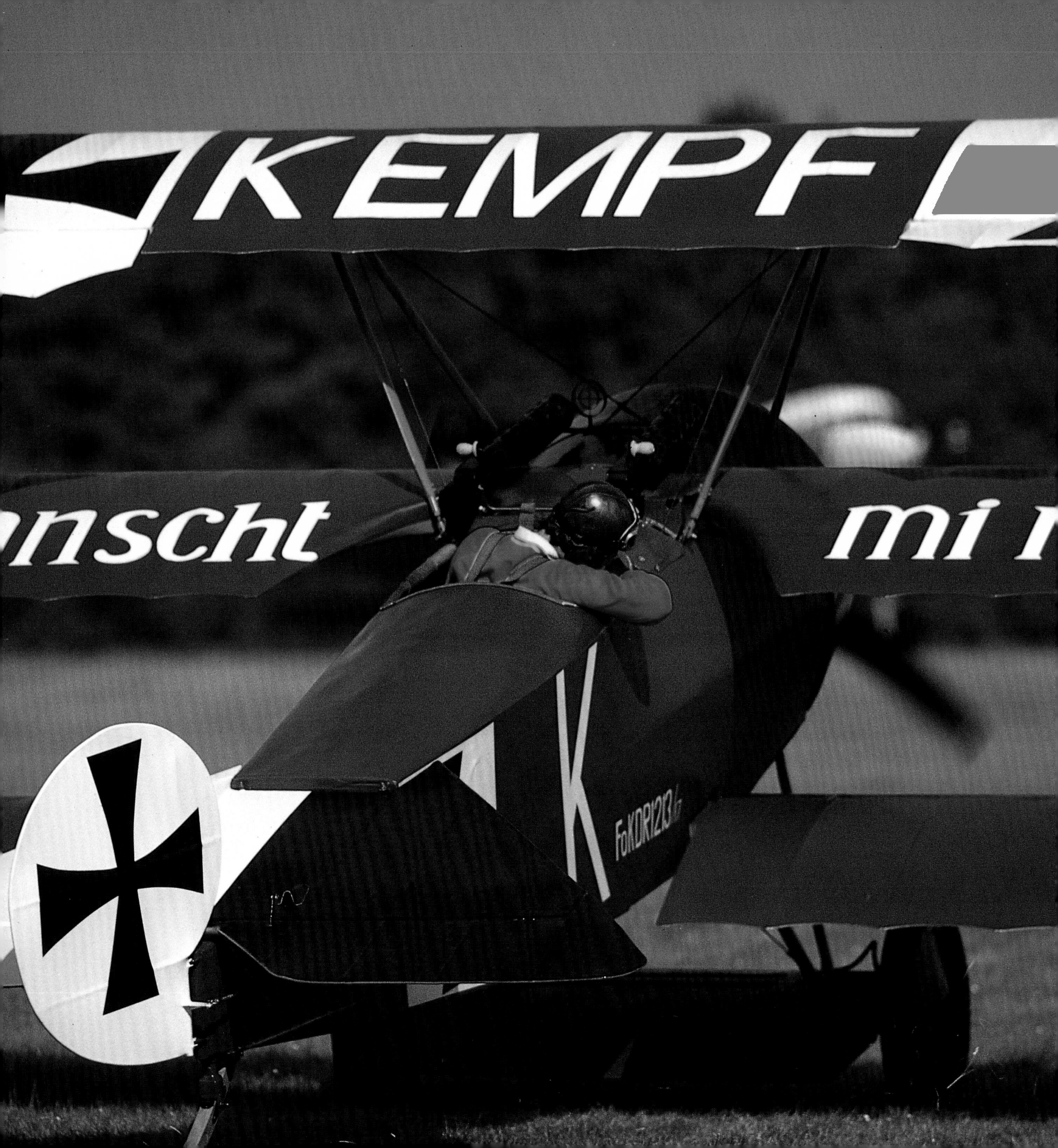
KEMPF

FIGHTERS

THE WORLD'S GREAT ACES AND THEIR PLANES

TEXT BY EDWARDS PARK

THOMASSON-GRANT

CHARLOTTESVILLE, VIRGINIA

Page 1 McDonnell Douglas F-15 Eagle.

Page 2 Dassault-Breguet *Rafale*.

Page 3 Replica, Curtiss D-III Headless biplane.

Page 4 Fokker Dr I *Dreidecker*.

Right Vought F4U-7 Corsair with the rondel of France's *Aéronavale*.

Published by Thomasson-Grant, Inc.
Design and photoediting by Leonard G. Phillips
Captions and editing by Owen Andrews
Copyright © 1990 by Thomasson-Grant, Inc. All rights reserved.
Photographs copyright © as credited on page 228.
This book, or any portions thereof, may not be reproduced in any form without written permission of Thomasson-Grant, Inc.
Printed and bound in Singapore by Tien Wah Press (Pte.) Ltd.

97 96 95 94 93 92 91 90   5 4 3 2 1

Library of Congress Cataloging-in-Publication Data
Park, Edwards.
Fighters : the world's great aces and their planes / by Edwards Park.
p.   cm.
ISBN 0-934738-65-3
1. Fighter plane combat–History. 2. Fighter planes–History.
3. Military history, Modern–20th century. 4. Fighter pilots–History. I. Title.
UG700.P37 1990
358.4'14'09–dc20   90-11093
                                            CIP

Thomasson-Grant, Inc.
One Morton Drive, Suite 500
Charlottesville, VA 22901
(804) 977-1780

TABLE OF CONTENTS

Dassault-Breguet Mirage F.1s.

INTRODUCTION

Four fighters appeared, very low on the horizon and coming fast. They clung so tightly together that they almost seemed one big awkward plane. But as they howled over the strip, propellers whipping dust from the steel matting, they broke apart, pulling sharply up and to the right, one after the other. Landing gear popped from beneath the lifting, banking wings, and the bellow of four big Allison engines changed to a harsh whistle as each sleek shape suddenly sprouted struts, wheels, fairings, and flaps, slashing and churning the air.

They half slipped around the pattern in a continuous curve, 200 yards between them. Still banking, the flight leader skimmed toward the end of the strip and flicked straight at the last moment, nose up, wheels groping for the matting. Then he landed with a tiny rattle, and the other three, coming behind him, reached down in the same way and touched the same spot.

We six replacements stood beside the strip in awed silence. This old squadron was suddenly our new home, and we had been advised to note its flying techniques by watching the last patrol come in. We'd never seen four planes land in such a hurry. I, for one, had a grand total of 42 hours on this dicey little fighter, the P-39. I had never shot its guns. I felt like an entrant in a six-day bike race who had barely given up his training wheels.

The planes rolled down the taxiway toward their revetments. One after another they passed us, handsome little creatures, drably dressed in a solid olive green or in green and tan splotches. Their undersides were pale gray; buff-colored paint covered each nose cone and the tops of the fins and flashed on the idly wheeling propeller blades.

Facing Curtiss P-40 Warhawk.

11

The pilots glanced down at us from their cockpits as they trundled by. I had an impression of yellow Mae Wests, a lot of straps, an assortment of flying helmets with goggles up and oxygen masks flapping below. And four intense young faces, shiny with sweat and begrimed with whirling dust.

Ludicrously awkward out of their element, the spluttering aircraft pivoted painfully into their separate revetments. One by one, the engines ran up with a little throat-clearing bark and then snapped into silence as their mixture controls were closed. We six walked quietly back to the alert shack, an open-walled shed with a grass-thatched roof, to meet the members of the family we had abruptly joined.

The commanding officer was a major, about 27 years old, taller than most of us—almost six feet—with crewcut hair and a black, droopy mustache. The operations officer had a small boy's face, thin and pale, with light blue eyes. The others, pleasant-looking college-boy types, were just rising from their games of bridge or solitaire, from their paperbacked novels, gathering their gear, relieved that the day's work was done and that they could board the jeeps and get back to camp.

All were very thin, for this was New Guinea, where food was scarce and bad, where dysentery was routine, where malaria and other exotic fevers did more damage than the enemy.

All were cordial to us newcomers; we represented tickets home for six of them— no one yet knew which six. We felt flattered by their questions about life in the States, the food we'd been eating, the new tunes on the radio, the things the girls were wearing. But when they talked among themselves that first evening, we were excluded. They chattered and joked with a startling intimacy, with apparently nothing too private, too sacred to be held back: Harry's bowel complaints, Pete's newly minted religious philosophy, Tommy's incredible sexual exploits on leave in Sydney, Roscoe's body parasites. We hadn't yet learned this language, so full of idiom, of buzz words, so larded with unselfconscious vulgarities.

Remembering our presence, they began to include us, talking now about their daily tasks, about what we would have to do alongside them. And listening, we could only conclude that they were putting us on. This was early in the war, and stateside flying schools didn't teach taking off in pairs or returning to base in that tightly locked echelon, down on the deck, which we had witnessed. It seemed impossible to fly fomation and yet look around endlessly at every patch of sky. It seemed absurd to perform violent maneuvers and sight and shoot the guns and still stay in formation.

We understood clearly that we could never ask how to do these things. Trained before Pearl Harbor, these old pilots knew nothing about the overcrowded, overworked new training programs back home. They'd simply have looked at us in despair and said, "Why are you here?"

Obviously, we could only survive and perhaps even become competent by learning everything we could, every second we could, on our own. To me, it seemed a lot more demanding than the four years I had spent at my tough old university.

So our acceptance into the squadron started in the cockpit. Next morning, I flew a two-plane weather flight over the Owen Stanley Range to check whether the morning mission—fighter escort for transports crammed with Australian infantry—could get through. I glued myself on the wing of a seasoned pilot and made the usual mistake

U.S. Navy Lieutenant Mark K. Bright in Grumman F6F Hellcat, USS *Lexington*, 1943.

of watching him too closely and the sky not closely enough. When he pointed upward without breaking radio silence, I looked—and saw the contrail of a Japanese observation plane, high above, far higher than any American plane could climb at that time. It was a gentle lesson in looking around. If that had been a Zero...

Next day I flew the mission itself as Red Two, tacked onto the wing of Red One, who was also that day's squadron leader. It was the safest spot the operations officer could find for me. I looked around more carefully, but forgot to switch from belly tank to main tank, so my engine quit. I dropped back momentarily, then restarted and got back into formation. Red Leader looked over at me and laughed. I laughed too and relaxed, and everything began to go more easily.

By the end of a month, four of us had become members of this most exclusive fraternity. The other two were dead.

"What are you going to do after the war?" we would often ask each other during bull sessions around the crude little bar we'd rigged up in a tent. The answers were disturbingly vague. We were good at only one thing—flying a single-engine, single-seat airplane and shooting machine guns from it. What could we possibly do in peacetime?

Those of us who joined up after Pearl Harbor were selected as fighter pilots because we were no taller than 5' 10", weighed no more than 160 pounds, had fast and decisive reactions, and were reasonably competent. Whether or not our instructors looked for something else, I cannot say. But we did share a capacity for recklessness.

In my case, coming from northern New England, I'd first discovered this streak when I skied. Even as a sprawling beginner, I'd sometimes inexplicably hurl myself down a slope, daring a spill, a broken leg. I never did break the leg because, along with the recklessness, I had a strong instinct for self-preservation.

I also learned as a kid that sometimes you had to resist that yen for safety and force yourself into a predicament that was just plain scary. Take the 30-foot diving platform. When I was about 10, I shinnied up there with a couple of other youngsters, and we huddled together, staring down at the lake so very far below. And finally, gulping down our dread, we jumped off one by one, grabbing our noses and hitting the water feet first. None of us liked it, but we knew it had to be done.

Growing boys have always experimented with daring and surviving, with facing up to frightening challenges. In my generation, if they also had perfect eyesight,

Vought F4U Corsair.

sound health, catlike reactions, the right physical dimensions, and above all a strong desire to fly, they very often became fighter pilots.

Flying World War II fighters, I think we all learned to think of recklessness as though it were a mechanical boost. We learned to turn it on the way a driver breaks out of cruise control when he passes a truck. Recklessness was right there in my plane's cockpit, ready to use when I needed it.

"Beaver leader, bandits three o'clock high!"

"I got 'em. Drop your tanks, boys!"

And each of us would instantly switch fuel feed to main tank, pull the release to drop off the 110-gallon belly tank we'd been using, twist the rheostat that turned on and brightened the gunsight, cram throttle and pitch control forward "right through the gate," and toggle the recklessness switch.

In the pioneering days of flight, everyone who crawled into a plane had first to turn on that inner switch. On December 17, 1903, Wilbur and Orville Wright shook hands quietly before Orville stretched out on the lower wing of the *Flyer*. Neither doubted for an instant that they would succeed in flying, yet they knew the risk they faced; they knew of all the lives already lost in the pursuit of flight.

Others who risked trying these awkward, unstable early flying machines were often professional daredevils—racing drivers, circus stunt men. The earliest military

Above Nieuport 28 of the American Expeditionary Force, 1918.

Facing General Dynamics F-16 Fighting Falcon.

pilots—among them my old commander, Hap Arnold—were a savvier breed: aware of the problems and dangers of flight, but determined to understand and control them, to make a future for this strange, wonderful invention.

Daredevils or innovators, these men—and women—needed the fighter pilot's controlled recklessness just to climb into any of the planes of 1914. They toggled that inner switch when they squeezed into the cockpits of their *Eindeckers* and Morane-Saulniers, their Albatroses and Nieuports and Gunbuses, their Fokker D VIIs and Spads and Sopwith Camels. They didn't realize it, but they were the prototypes of a special breed that would flourish for decades after they were gone, that would fight another war, that would, in the late years of their century, take on more power and speed than humans could manage without the steadying hand of science at the controls.

Fighter pilots all. They started as just pilots. They're now the human part of the computer system that flies F-16s and MiG-23s and other craft belonging as much to space as to air.

Fighter pilots. They're not quite yet extinct.

Replica, Curtiss D-III Headless biplane.

FIRST OF THE FIGHTERS

Considering how many years mankind spent trying to devise a flying machine, the triumphant hum of the Wright *Flyer* in 1903 took a surprisingly long time to echo around the world. For five years after their breakthrough at Kitty Hawk, Orville and Wilbur were all but forgotten by the press. Reclusive by nature, the brothers didn't make good copy. More colorful aviation headlines came from France, where wealthy adventurers toyed with flying.

Then, late in the summer of 1908, the Wrights demonstrated a new generation of airplanes on both sides of the Atlantic. While Orville put the new *Flyer* through its paces before skeptical Army officers at Fort Myer, Virginia, Wilbur stunned European aviators with a series of exhibitions near Paris. Suddenly aviation was *hot,* and everyone—including royalty—lionized the Wrights and every other flight pioneer they could find, including the Wrights' American rival, Glenn Curtiss, and all the leading aviators of Europe: Hubert Latham, Gabriel Voisin, Henri Farman, A.V. Roe, and many others from France, Germany, England, and Italy. Among the heroes were the recent conqueror of the English Channel, Louis Blériot, and Alberto Santos-Dumont, the first European (he was originally from Brazil) to fly.

The military possibilities of aircraft intrigued many of the government figures who came to watch the air shows. The Continent was slipping ever closer to a major war, and Great Britain, France, Germany, Italy, Austria, and Russia quickly set up special aviation branches with military units formed of Caudrons, Farmans, Voisins, Vickers, Aviatiks, Rumplers, and many other types, with national colors painted on canvas and linen or flapping from spruce spars or wire stays. In the States, the Wrights sold a model to the U.S. Army Signal Corps. So did Glenn Curtiss and Glenn L. Martin.

Not long after, planes began appearing in warfare. In 1911, as Italy was

Above On July 25, 1909, in his Type XI monoplane, Louis Blériot (right) became the first man to fly across the English Channel. The 36-minute flight brought fame to Blériot and profits to his company. For England, long shielded from Continental aggressors by the waters of the Channel, his feat also portended a new kind of military threat.

Facing The Caudron G-3 flew reconnaissance missions in World War I. Like many other early aircraft, it used a rotary engine, whose air-cooled cylinders spun around the central shaft with the propeller. The rotary was lighter than liquid-cooled engines, but the heavy, rapidly spinning cylinders also generated a lot of torque, making planes unpredictable in flight.

Above The cockpit of the Blériot XI shows the typically sparse instrumentation of its time. But beneath the copper oil and fuel tanks, any pilot will recognize the controls. The Type XI was, in fact, one of the first planes to use what has been the standard configuration ever since: a stick to control elevators and wing-warping (later ailerons), and a bar underfoot for the rudder.

Right As the sole pilot of General Obregón's air force, and one of the few combat pilots anywhere in 1913, Didier Masson patrolled the Mexican coast in a Curtiss pusher biplane. He resigned his Mexican commission when World War I broke out and went to France, where he flew reconnaissance in Caudrons and pursuit missions in Nieuports. He transferred to the Lafayette Escadrille in 1916 and gained renown both for his flying skills and the delicious meals he organized in the officers' mess. Toward the end of the war (which he survived), he trained new American pilots in Nieuports.

fighting to take Libya from the Turkish Empire, Italian pilot Carlo Piazza flew a Blériot on a reconnaissance flight from Tripoli to Aziza—apparently the world's first combat mission. Another Italian pilot was soon dropping hand-held bombs on Turkish targets at Taguira and Ain Zara. In 1913, the French bombed targets in Morocco, and two Bulgarians in a German-built *Taube* dropped four hand-held bombs on a Turkish base at Adrianople.

Later in 1913, General Alvaro Obregón, leader of one of Mexico's many political factions, hired an American professional pilot, Didier Masson, to run his air force in his struggle with another faction leader, General Victoriano Huerta. The Obregón air force consisted of one Curtiss plane. Its mission: destroy the Huerta navy— a single gunboat, creaking with old age. Masson flew over this target several times, dropping fused tin cans packed with gunpowder. He didn't destroy anything except a few siestas, but two years later, when he volunteered for French military service and wangled his way into the flying corps, he could claim prewar experience in combat flying.

Huerta later started his own air force with 50 aviators and 24 planes. One of the pilots, an American named Phil Rader, got into an air battle with yet another Yank, Dean Lamb, representing the air force of yet another faction leader, General Carranza. Lamb and Rader blazed away at each other with pistols—quite harmlessly.

As the probability of a major European war grew larger, so did the fame of a dashing young Frenchman, Roland Garros. Born on the Indian Ocean island of Réunion, Garros came to Paris to study music, but fell for the glamorous adventure of flight. The great Santos-Dumont took him on as a student, and then Garros gained his

own measure of greatness. In 1913, he became the first man to pilot a plane across the Mediterranean, and he won air races from Paris to Rome and Madrid.

He joined Morane-Saulnier, one of the world's earliest aircraft firms, and he toured Europe and America with his company's handsome little monoplanes, showing off their performance. The summer of 1914 found him the toast of Germany with his acrobatic demonstrations.

Garros was starring in Berlin on August 3 when war was declared, and that evening he attended a German celebration. Most of Europe, ironically, rejoiced at the outbreak of the war which would kill and maim millions. The Frenchman knew he faced internment if he didn't get out of Berlin. Feigning drunkenness, he headed for a bathroom, opened a window, and slipped out in the darkness. He made for the airfield and found his plane—well guarded by German police.

The reality of war hadn't yet asserted itself. The glamorous French aviator was a hero to the guards, and when he asked permission to roll out his plane, they probably helped. He collared some extra fuel cans and swung the propeller himself. As the rotary engine barked into life, he managed to climb onto a moving wing and into the cockpit. And so, in a time when no one risked flying at night, Garros took off in the dark—no instruments, mind you—and got clean away. Learning of his escape, the German press

Blériot sold large numbers of his Type XI and successive models to the fledgling air forces of England and France. Fitted with more powerful engines to keep ahead of competitors, a number of his monoplanes disintegrated and crashed. The cause was simple—the planes' frames weren't capable of withstanding flight stresses over 50 miles per hour. Blériot tried strengthening his designs, but in military minds, a preference for apparently sturdier biplanes developed which would persist into the 1930s.

Above A *Taube*, or "dove," named for its birdlike wings, flew the first aerial bombing mission in history during Italy's 1911 campaign in Turkish-held Libya. Designed by Austrian Igo Etrich in 1910, the *Taube* was the most common German aircraft type when World War I began. Twenty different firms constructed variants; the best was made by Rumpler, the firm that bought Etrich's patents.

Right The 1912 Deperdussin was the first plane to fly at over 100 miles per hour. Louis Bechereau, who was to guide the development of the great wartime Spads, designed the Deperdussin with a remarkably streamlined monocoque frame made of thin veneers of tulipwood. An innovative twin-rotary engine—a double ring of whirling cylinders—delivered 140 horsepower.

Above The 1910 Hanriot, one of many French monoplanes that emerged in response to Blériot's successes, flew at speeds of up to 70 miles per hour. In World War I, the Hanriot firm would build a very capable biplane, the HD-1. Willy Coppens, Belgium's leading ace, scored many of his 37 victories in the HD-1.

suggested that his entire three-week tour had been a ruse to allow him to spy out preparations for war.

Landing at intervals to refuel from his supply, Garros made it south to Switzerland and then across into France. In Paris, he volunteered for service and was sent to Escadrille M.S. 23. The number of each French squadron was supplemented by the type of aircraft it flew: "M.S." stood for Morane-Saulnier. Garros was right at home with his pet monoplanes, joining a number of well-known peacetime pilots. One of them, Adolphe Pégoud, had wrenched a plane around in the world's first loop the year before.

Garros got into action in the fall of 1914, after the First Battle of the Marne. The squadron's job, of course, was observation, and when the flyers spotted German planes doing the same thing, many simply waved. They were all pilots together, often knew each other from the prewar flying circuit, and the act of flying was surely dangerous enough for everyone without adding the extra dimension of shooting guns back and forth.

Roland Garros and his friend Raymond Saulnier take the credit for making the first machine gun synchronizer that brought down an enemy plane in combat. Several patents for similar devices had been filed by French and German inventors before the war. All were deficient, and Garros' solution, armored wedges on the propeller, was a temporary (and dangerous) compromise, not part of a true synchronizer. The firing gun's vibrations and the impact of bullets on the propeller deflectors severely stressed the frame of his Morane-Saulnier Parasol. And if the wedges failed, Garros would shoot off the propeller and lose control of the plane.

But Roland Garros was a fire-eater, angry at the Huns for having accused him of spying. He packed a pistol when he flew, and when he first met the enemy—a couple of Germans in an Aviatik—he whizzed up alongside and flew wing to wing. The Germans waved cheerily. Garros steadied his revolver on the edge of his cockpit and got off six shots.

No luck. The Germans were unhit but outraged, and Garros angrily broke for home. On subsequent missions, he again tried firing his pistol, but he couldn't hit a thing. His little M.S. simply danced around too much.

Garros wasn't alone in his haste to down enemy aircraft. Three weeks after war was declared, three British planes boxed in a *Taube* and forced it to land by threatening to slice its tail off with a propeller. The first kill in the air was credited to two Frenchmen, Sergeant Joseph Frantz and Corporal Louis Quénault. Flying a Voisin pusher with a Hotchkiss machine gun mounted by the observer's seat, they shot down a German Aviatik B in early October. Alexander Azakov, soon to be Russia's leading ace, tried lowering a grapnel onto a German Albatros. That didn't work, so he rammed the fellow instead (a tactic the Russians revived in World War II) and sent him down. The British suggested using an old-fashioned blunderbuss which would spray a lot of projectiles in the general direction of an enemy, and a French pilot took a shot with one at a German plane. Hand grenades were sometimes dropped, plane to plane. And little darts—

fléchettes—were occasionally showered down upon enemy aircraft in those early days.

But every single-seater pilot knew that to be really effective, he needed a machine gun that he could aim by flying his plane at his target. With a gun like this, the entire plane would become a kind of weapon and the pilot would truly be a *fighter* pilot.

Soon after the war started, machine guns appeared on heavy two-seater biplanes, and by the beginning of 1915, single-seater biplanes were beginning to carry Hotchkiss guns mounted on the upper wing so the bullets would clear the propeller. But the recoil put dangerous stress on the wing and its slender struts. If only there were a way to mount a gun on the plane's nose, to fire through the propeller disk without shooting the blades off...

Roland Garros learned that experiments had been made just before the war with a synchronizer that would stop the machine gun from firing when a propeller blade was in the way. Raymond Saulnier himself, Garros' old employer, had tried the device. Unfortunately, faulty ammunition sometimes made the gun hang fire, and the delayed bullet would then smash through one of the whirling propeller blades anyway.

Raymond Garros made his career in Morane-Saulnier monoplanes like the Type H (shown in replica) and the Type L or "Parasol," so named because its single wing hung jauntily over the cockpit. Garros flew a predecessor of the Type H across the Mediterranean and mounted his famous machine gun in the Type L. Both were powered by the Gnome 80-horsepower rotary engine and were known as agile but tricky to fly.

Saulnier met this problem by affixing little steel triangles on the propeller blades just where bullets would strike. This sent some of the bullets whining off to the side and left the blades intact.

Garros talked to Saulnier about this apparatus, wangled permission from army authorities to try it, found the iron wedges unstable, beefed up the attachment, and finally mounted a Hotchkiss gun on the nose of a new Morane-Saulnier monoplane. He had to wait until April Fool's Day 1915 before the miserable winter weather eased off enough to test the gun in combat.

In the air, Garros spotted some German two-seaters flying too high to be in danger from any French two-seaters laden with machine guns. But they weren't too high for the world's first fighter plane. He climbed up to them and approached one from the side. Since no monoplane had ever carried a machine gun, the German pilot and observer paid scant attention.

Garros slipped into an attack curve that brought him "into the hip pocket"—right on the target's tail. Then he opened fire.

The Hotchkiss worked well, but Garros found hitting another plane, even when you're "at his six o'clock," isn't all that easy. The German, who had expected nothing but perhaps a friendly wave, desperately dove and twisted. Garros used up two five-second drums of ammo before he scored. The German crumpled and fell. Roland Garros had become the father of all fighter pilots.

Over the next four weeks, he shot down five more planes before he was hit by ground fire while making a low pass over a train. His fuel line was cut, his engine quit, and he dead-sticked his little fighter to a landing behind German lines. Unhurt, he tried to burn his plane, but God was smiling on the Kaiser that day, for the fire never took. Instead, the plane was captured, and its machine gun thoroughly studied.

Garros, too, was taken as he tried to reach the Dutch border. Realizing that they had a notable captive, the Germans guarded him well and moved him about. Nevertheless, the French daredevil managed to escape in 1918, and somehow he made it to England. He got back in the air, flew for nine months, and then, a scant five weeks before Armistice was signed, went down in flames.

A Fokker D VII got him. Considered the ultimate fighter of the war, it carried twin Spandau machine guns mechanically timed to shoot through the propeller. Aerial warfare had come a long way from steel-wedge synchronization and left Roland Garros behind, "hoist by his own petard."

Facing Ironically, the French Morane-Saulnier Type H (shown in replica) was the prototype for the first true German fighter. Anthony Fokker, a Dutch airplane manufacturer, obtained a Type H in France in 1913 and built a copy, which he called the M5K and sold as a light scout. After the Germans brought Garros' firing mechanism to Fokker in 1915, he mounted his improved version on an M5K. Rechristened the E I *Eindecker*, the previously unremarkable little plane would terrorize Allied air forces in the fall of 1915.

FOKKER SCOURGE

The Germans made the most of Roland Garros' failure to get a fire going on his downed Morane-Saulnier. They studied the steel deflectors that had allowed the Frenchman to shoot through his propeller arc and tried to copy them. The tests were a disaster. Firing steel-jacketed bullets at a higher velocity than Garros' Hotchkiss, the German machine guns quickly smashed the deflecting wedges and shot off the propeller blades. The whole contraption was bundled off to Anthony Fokker to see what he could do about it.

Fokker, a 25-year-old Dutch engineer and airplane builder who had learned his trade in Germany, looked over the Garros gun system. Recalling a prewar device, he designed a cam that would interrupt the firing of a machine gun synchronously with the rotation of the propellers. He mounted the new gun on his new monoplane, the *Eindecker*, and tested it on the ground. Perfect! "Now try it in combat with a real plane," said the German authorities.

So Tony Fokker, civilian, found himself in a German pilot's uniform, carrying phony officer's identification papers to prevent his being shot as a spy if captured. Feeling a bit uneasy, he flew off to hunt for an Allied plane. At last he spotted a two-seater Farman grinding along straight and level, but he couldn't make himself fire. He knew his gun would work. To fire it would be simple murder—by a neutral.

When Fokker landed and explained his feelings, the German pilots understood. They welcomed the new gun-equipped *Eindeckers* and went hunting without a qualm. Soon they were scoring victories.

One Fokker *Eindecker* went to *Leutnant* Oswald Boelcke. He was one of five brothers, the sons of a teacher. Close family bonds drew him after an older brother, Wilhelm, into an army career. He liked being a cadet and became an officer in communications—a field closely linked with the new career of aviation. Young Boelcke began learning to fly before the war, and at the First Battle of the Marne in September

Above Like many early airplane manufacturers, Anthony Fokker was a pilot daring enough to fly his own designs, a mechanic skilled at quickly adapting and improving others' ideas, and a businessman with a talent for hiring good assistants. Twenty-four years old when he put the E I *Eindecker* together, he was also the youngest of the major airplane manufacturers.

Facing Anthony Fokker's firing device and the flying skill of men like Oswald Boelcke and Max Immelman gave the fragile, underpowered *Eindecker* the edge it enjoyed for a few months in 1915 and 1916.

Max Immelman was the second German to down an Allied plane from an *Eindecker* (right), and as his score mounted, he became a national hero. "Immelman shoots faster than one can write," said Kaiser Wilhelm when he learned, while preparing a letter of congratulations on Immelman's twelfth victory, that the pilot had just shot down a thirteenth enemy plane.

1914 he was piloting an observation plane.

He often had Wilhelm with him as an observer. The story goes that when Wilhelm was shipped to another outfit, both complained, and Oswald was grounded for a spell to get over his pique. This experience seems to have hardened him into a disciplinarian, tough on himself and devoted to the idea of teamwork. Meeting a French or British plane, he'd swing his new-model, gun-equipped L.V.G. into positions which always gave his observer a shot.

Aggressiveness and leadership earned Boelcke the chance to try out one of Tony Fokker's new *Eindeckers*. He scored early and often, learning to fly his little plane instinctively, to slide into a position from which he couldn't miss, always being sure of a kill. He also had the knack, perhaps inherited from his father, for teaching, for passing on his techniques to other pilots.

One of the novitiates who learned at Boelcke's knee was a handsome, black-eyed youth named Max Immelman. His name passed into the language of aviation because of a maneuver he allegedly perfected, the "Immelman turn": a half roll on top of a half loop.

We used it in World War II—a quick and rather startling method of gaining altitude and changing direction at the same time. In a fast and agile fighter like the Japanese Zero, an Immelman could be formidable to face. Old P-39 pilots of my own

New Guinea squadron used to tell us replacements how Zeroes would take off far below, "pull an Immelman," while their wheels were still retracting, and then roll out dead ahead, coming straight at the Airacobras, guns ablaze. The old guys were probably putting us on. An Immelman on takeoff seems too much even for the fabulous Zero. Still...

Certainly Max Immelman never could have wrenched a Fokker E II (top speed about 82 miles per hour) into such a maneuver without stalling, spinning, and probably losing the wings. The true Immelman turn was probably a *chandelle*, which young pilots still learn, a steeply climbing 180-degree turn.

Anyway, Max Immelman, like Boelcke, had been a cadet, taken a commission, and was serving in a railroad regiment when war broke out. He managed a transfer to flight school and got through it, though he had trouble with his landings (the only distinction Immelman and I shared!).

At last he was posted to a reconnaissance squadron and became good enough for an *Eindecker* squadron, where he came under Boelcke's tutelage. Soon he was habitually flying beside Boelcke, forming the world's first two-man team—what would later be called an "element."

The two Germans, however, had no concept of today's element tactics—two planes attacking together. Their combats were individual match-ups, and they were both so successful at these dogfights that they formed the nucleus of what the Allies called "The Fokker Scourge." Through most of 1915, no French or British plane could dominate the Fokkers. Immelman and Boelcke rolled up their scores, competing in a friendly way with each other. With eight victories apiece, they were decorated by the Kaiser with the distinctive old *Pour le Mérite*, which has since been dubbed "The Blue Max."

Boelcke and Immelman set the pattern for all the fighter pilots who followed them: controlled recklessness, great skill, desire, and what flyer-author Mike Spick in his thoughtful book *The Ace Factor* calls "situational awareness": knowing exactly what is going on in three dimensions and where you fit in. Yet in many ways the two were an odd couple.

Oswald Boelcke, ever the teacher, considered flying a fighter an exercise in scholarship. He studied fighter tactics, he noted weaknesses in German designs and training, and he recommended improvements. He seems to have put himself above the

One of Oswald Boelcke's more notable victories was over Victor Chapman, a member of the Lafayette Escadrille and the first American killed in air combat. Boelcke shot Chapman down on June 23, only five days after losing his best pilot, Max Immelman, in a mêlée with some British FE-2bs. On October 28, Boelcke himself would die, losing control of his Albatros D I after one of his "cubs" accidently collided with it. With him, the German air force lost not only a skilled fighter pilot, but its most thoughtful and farsighted aviation strategist.

Fokker continually updated the *Eindecker* until he had exhausted the potential of its prewar frame and wingwarping controls. An 80-horsepower Oberursel rotary engine drove the E I at about 70 miles per hour, and an improved 100-horsepower Oberursel pushed the E II up to 85 mph. Twin air-cooled Spandau machine guns doubled firepower on the E III (shown in replica), but their extra weight made the plane less agile. Trying to keep ahead of the fast new French Nieuport 11, Fokker loaded down the disastrous E IV with a 160-horsepower twin rotary and *three* machine guns, the burden of which virtually shook the little scout to pieces.

adulation that the German press poured upon Immelman as the pair kept on scoring, concerning himself only with the job at hand. He remained a humanist, not afraid to laugh, generous to others, including his enemies.

This athletic, heavily handsome German had been a fine swimmer in prewar days. When a French boy fell into a canal in an occupied village and was thrashing about helplessly, Boelcke dove in, rescued him, scolded him for not learning to swim, and went on about his business. The villagers tried to get him an official reward, but of course the French government wouldn't go along with honoring one of *les sales Boches*.

Boelcke's letters home indicate true regret whenever he killed an adversary. He preferred simply shooting his opponent down, then paying him a visit in hospital, perhaps with a bottle of champagne.

Max Immelman was ever the student. Despite his dashing little mustache and dancing black eyes, he had a reputation for near asceticism, abstaining from tobacco, red meat, strong drink, and loose women. Instead, he found his pleasure in striving for absolute perfection at his task. He and Boelcke worked out the "Fokker bounce": get above your target; dive from where you're hardest to see, out of the sun if you can; pass astern of your target, picking up speed; then, when you're beneath him, where he can't see you, haul your nose up and cut loose at his vulnerable belly.

Obviously, a sharp, climbing turn—an Immelman turn—after the attack would put you in position for a second pass if you needed it. Immelman generally didn't. His fame mounted with his score. Germans almost worshipped the "Eagle of Lille," and when finally he was killed in June 1916, the German Empire mourned.

The Allies had by then come up with answers to the Fokkers that had effectively ruled the sky. Biplanes arrived at the front, went into action, and were often quickly replaced by better models. Britain at first stayed with pusher planes, which allowed a clear field of fire for their machine guns. There was the famous F.E. 2b, called the "Fee," an improvement on its near twin, the Vickers F.B. 5, or "Gunbus." Both were two-seaters. A single-seat pusher, the de Havilland D.H. 2, showed up soon after the Fee. Then came a tractor plane (propeller in front) with a synchronized gun: the Sopwith 1¹/₂ Strutter, so called because of the arrangement of its wing struts. France produced a typically beautiful little tractor scout, the Nieuport 11, aptly dubbed "*Bébé*," with a Lewis gun fixed atop the upper wing to clear the propeller arc. This was soon followed by a new

and improved model, the Nieuport 17. All had powerful engines, and all could outperform Tony Fokker's *Eindeckers*.

On an evening mission shortly before the Battle of the Somme, Immelman was patrolling with some other Fokkers when they tangled with a couple of Fees. They whirled around in what my squadron used to call a "soirée," and Immelman's plane suddenly came apart. The reason wasn't clear. Other German pilots said it simply disintegrated.

Aghast, the German people mourned their hero and refused to believe that he could have been shot down by another plane. Surely a lucky shot from the ground had caught him, or perhaps his gun synchronizer had failed, causing him to chew off a propeller blade. Vibration then could have shaken the plane to bits. On the other hand, the Royal Flying Corps reported that during the dogfight that evening one of its Fee gunners had got a clear shot and clobbered an *Eindecker*.

Anyway, the dashing Eagle of Lille was gone, and Oswald Boelcke, depressed at the loss of his friend, was shipped off on detached service and then given command of a squadron. This gave Boelcke his chance to teach. He trained the young pilots assigned to his *jagsdstaffel* ("*jasta*" for short), rehearsing them in all the techniques he knew. Hide in the sun, he told them; get too close to miss before you open fire; know where you are and where other planes are all the time; turn toward an attack, not away. His precepts came to be known as the "Dicta Boelcke."

He set out to form his "cubs" into an elite squadron, keeping them out of combat until they were ready. He still flew himself, taking off alone every morning, and when he'd landed, he'd stride into the mess hall for breakfast and face that inevitable question,

The success of the de Havilland D.H. 2 and other British pusher-type fighters of early 1916 showed that it took more than a synchronized gun to make a formidable fighter. Despite its looks, the single-seat D.H. 2 was maneuverable and light; a 100-horsepower Gnome engine (similar to the E III's Oberursel, a derivative design) propelled it a tad faster than the *Eindecker*. Lanoe Hawker, the RFC's first ace, was flying a D.H. 2 when he battled Manfred von Richthofen, whose Albatros was a far better plane. Hawker, however, was a better pilot, and the baron pursued him through 50 turns and fired hundreds of rounds before he brought him down.

traditionally put to generations of fighter pilots as they returned from a mission—or from a leave: "Did you get any?"

Often Boelcke would answer with another question: "Is my chin black?" And if it was, the cubs would know that their hero's chin, the only exposed part of his face, had been stained by blown-back smoke from his gun. A black chin meant he had fired. And if Boelcke fired, he scored. He hated wasting ammunition.

The *jasta* was equipped with a beautiful new German fighter, the Albatros. Constructed of plywood, it went better than 100 miles per hour and carried twin synchronized Spandaus. Boelcke saw that everyone racked up some time on this splendid machine, then felt that they were ready for action.

In its first fight, Boelcke's *jasta* shot down two British bombers and four Fees. When more British planes closed in, the German C.O. yanked his lads out of trouble. From then on, the unit scored and scored—a hot outfit if ever there was one. One member was a rather cold-blooded young Prussian aristocrat named Manfred von Richthofen. He had trouble getting started, but everyone felt he showed promise.

On an October day in 1916, after most of the Battle of the Somme had petered out in a useless and hideous bath of blood, *Hauptmann* Oswald Boelcke took off with Richthofen, Erwin Böhme, and three other pilots to intercept some British planes—a mission that we in our later war would call a "scramble." They spotted the enemy, a couple of de Havillands, and tore in. And in the attack, Boelcke and his good friend Böhme collided.

It wasn't bad—a gentle brushing together of the two Albatroses—but both planes glided away, out of action. Böhme nursed his back to his base and managed to crash-land, turning turtle on his damaged landing gear. But he, like others, had seen Boelcke, the C.O., the father figure, gradually nose down into a steep dive and finally smash into the shell-cratered earth.

And so died one of the war's first true fighter pilots, and perhaps the most important of them all. Boelcke's carefully considered reports on planes and tactics shaped German thinking for 20 years and rubbed off on military flyers in every land. When my friends and I flew in the Pacific, many things that helped us do our jobs, and often survive, we owed to the skillful, careful, thoughtful, thoroughly decent Oswald Boelcke—an enemy flyer in a long-ago war.

Facing With the Albatros series of 1916 and 1917, the Germans regained their aerial advantage. All the Albatroses, from the D I and D II of 1916 to the D Va of 1917 and 1918 (shown in replica), featured a sleek plywood monocoque shell, a six-cylinder water-cooled Mercedes engine, and twin synchronized Spandau machine guns. More powerful engines increased the speed of the D III and D Va, and a narrower (but weaker) lower wing improved visibility. In the D III, the best of the series, Richthofen scored 35 of his 80 victories.

THE BRITISH ADVENTURE

Before the Great War, when the airplane was still a madcap experiment, aviators of all nations were universally foolhardy. But attitudes about flying differed slightly from nation to nation. Planes fascinated the French, and kid-gloved gentlemen were often lured into climbing aboard and having a go. German aristocrats tended to think of pilots as grease-smudged aerial chauffeurs. The British gentry embraced aviation as an adventurous and exclusive sport.

So, when war broke out, the pilots of French Farmans and Morane-Saulniers were often wealthy boulevardiers; Garros, for example, was a rich lawyer's son. The Germans who piloted Rumpler and L.V.G. reconnaissance planes were noncommissioned technicians, outranked by the lieutenants and captains in the observer's seat. And whatever their social background, the young officers of the Royal Flying Corps who ferried Britain's first warplanes across the English Channel shared the sportsman's lighthearted outlook and healthy desire to win.

This last urge was well nourished by Hugh Trenchard, the ex-cavalry officer who soon became the RFC's commanding general. Trenchard clearly saw what warplanes could and should do and had no inhibitions about pressing his points loudly and stubbornly before Britain's politicians.

"Boom" Trenchard had no use for red tape, and little for civilian sensibilities. Once, on assignment in London, wearing civvies, he was approached by a female superpatriot who looked at him coldly and asked why he wasn't wearing a war badge, indicating service.

Trenchard stared back at her balefully. "And where, Madame, is your war baby?" he boomed.

In 1918, Trenchard's air arm became the Royal Air Force. Like Billy Mitchell

Above Major Hugh Trenchard commanded the Royal Flying Corps throughout World War I. Even in the dark days of late 1915, when the RFC had no plane that could match the *Eindecker*, Trenchard sought ways to maintain a strong British air presence. Formation tactics, he found, were the best way to compensate for the weaknesses of individual planes. He served the RFC well on the home front, too, consistently anticipating its future needs, energetically lobbying for the funds to provide better planes, more manpower, and more training.

Facing The Sopwith Camel of 1917 (shown in replica) gave RFC flyers a vehicle in which they could effectively apply the lessons of aerial combat. It was in a Camel that Canadian Roy Brown shot down Richthofen, and altogether, this deft and useful ship accounted for 1,294 German planes—more than any other Allied fighter. Like the P-51 of World War II, the Camel was no mount for a novice; the torque generated by its 130-horsepower rotary engine made it difficult to handle. But in experienced hands, it maneuvered very sharply, and its twin synchronized machine guns—Britain's first— had the firepower to match the twin Spandaus of Albatroses and Fokker *Dreideckers*.

The pace of aircraft development in World War I was so rapid that a design often went into production just as its day was passing. The Royal Aircraft Factory FE-8, the last of the British pusher fighters, arrived at the front too late to be as useful as doughty predecessors like the Vickers Gunbus, the FE-2b, and the D.H. 2.

in the United States, he strove after the war to keep his force well armed. And when, 22 years after it had been formed, the RAF rewarded his foresight by defeating Hitler's Luftwaffe in the Battle of Britain, Trenchard was there to boom his congratulations, to shout his demands for more planes, more flyers, more training.

The British flyers of 1914 had little training and primitive aircraft. But they were rich in personality. Britain has always suffered eccentrics gladly, and the infant Royal Flying Corps had its share of strange characters.

One, indeed, was named Louis Strange. His fetish: machine guns. Setting off for France, he bolted an air-cooled Lewis gun to the forward cockpit of his Farman. The awkward biplane, a mass of struts and wires shoved protestingly through the air by a puny Gnome rotary engine, didn't take kindly to the added weight. Lieutenant Strange made it to France, but when he and his gunner scrambled after a German plane cruising at 5,000 feet, they found their top ceiling, after a tedious climb, was 3,500 feet. The gunner sprayed the sky. The German didn't deign to notice.

Strange tried mounting his Lewis on an Avro 504, which had the power to handle the weight, and other Allied pilots picked up the idea. When Strange's squadron got hold of a single-seater—a Martinsyde Scout with a machine gun mounted on the upper wing to clear the propeller—Strange appropriated it.

A jammed ammunition drum on the gun almost undid him. He had met a German plane and fired all the drum's 47 shots without effect. Flying with his knees, he rose up in the cockpit to yank the empty drum out of the gun and shove a new one in. But the stuck drum stayed stuck. Strange stood up to tug harder, lost control of the plane, and when it stalled and spun, he fell out. Pilots didn't wear safety belts then.

Strange held on to that stupid drum. Now praying that it *wouldn't* come loose, he managed to hoist his legs back into the cockpit, kick his way out of the spin, and head for the barn.

James McCudden got to France about as early as Strange, but as an air mechanic. Being a good sort of chap—RFC equivalent to having "the right stuff"—McCudden began to fly as an observer-gunner, then returned to England for pilot training. Back in France, he flew a Fee with a Rolls-Royce engine and scored his first victories in it. It was so stable he could stand up in his cockpit to look over the tail, to the consternation of his observer-gunner in the forward seat. As McCudden was doing this one time, his glove blew off, slammed into the pusher propeller, and broke a blade. He managed to land before vibration tore the ship apart.

That was a problem with pushers. When things come loose in an open cockpit, the wind carries them backward—and in a pusher, that's where the prop is. To keep ejected cartridges from hitting the prop, diaperlike bags hung around the guns of Fees, Gunbuses, and D.H. 2s. McCudden started a loop one day, changed his mind, and pushed forward out of his upward zoom. Of course everything in the cockpit flew into the air, including a spare cartridge drum which struck the prop. Three of the four blades turned to sawdust, and one tailboom snapped. As soon as McCudden sat down in a field, the poor, broken Fee fell apart.

James McCudden (top) could well appreciate the flying characteristics of the S.E. 5 (top and above). As observer or pilot, he flew in the Morane-Saulnier Parasol, the F.E. 2, the D.H. 2, and the Sopwith Scout, or "Pup." Flying the S.E. 5a for the first time in 1917, he said: "Although it flew rather strangely, I liked the machine immensely, as it was very fast after the Sopwith Scout, and one could see out of it so thoroughly well." McCudden saw clearly enough to bring down more than 30 Germans with the S.E. 5's Lewis machine gun. Placed over the wing, the gun fired 97 rounds from its drum feed, was yanked down the curved Foster mount for reloading, and had a ring-and-ball sight between the center wing struts.

The Sopwith Scout, designed by Herbert Smith, had excellent handling characteristics—it has been called "the finest flying machine of the First World War." Like many British fighters of 1915 and 1916, it was built around the Le Rhone 80-horsepower engine; its chief drawback was that engine's lack of power compared with German contemporaries like the 160-horsepower Albatros. When more powerful rotaries became available, Smith came up with the superb Sopwith Camel, whose lines clearly showed its descent from the agile Pup.

McCudden went on from the slow, stable pushers to the "tractors," the hottest planes of the day. The S.E. 5 could reach 10,000 feet in eight minutes and indicate 136 miles per hour at that altitude. A generation later, I learned to fly on a Stearman PT-17 primary trainer which couldn't match that performance.

Perhaps because McCudden had started as a mechanic, he treated flying as a craft instead of a sport. He worked at it like a shoemaker, producing victories rather than boots. He liked to fly alone and hunt German observation planes. Climbing high in his Sopwith Pup, and later his S.E. 5, he'd spot the Boches at lower altitudes and quickly close on them. He methodically built up his score, endlessly tuning his planes and his guns, analyzing his combats, chewing himself out when he made mistakes or picked up a couple of bullet holes. Always he tried for the perfect flight, where common sense would temper his aggression and nothing would go wrong.

McCudden was deeply shocked in one combat when he hit a German Albatros and it caught fire. He had never really thought that enemy planes had fellow humans in them until he saw that pilot thrashing in agony as he fell in flames. To become a great ace, the British craftsman had to steel himself to the fact of killing. He died in a crash only four months before the Armistice, when his engine quit on takeoff. Instead of following the procedure he himself had so often taught—never turn back to the field—he tried to get back for a forced landing, and his plane spun in. That shouldn't have happened to a pilot so self-demanding. But it did. It still does.

McCudden the perfectionist held one squadron mate in deep awe: Albert Ball. Even today, Ball stirs wonder. He was still in his teens when he made his name as an outstanding ace, and he never grew up enough to act the role of a killer.

A small, high-strung lad, Ball had the face of a child and traits that were more childish than simply eccentric. One was patriotism—for Ball, a religion that produced what could only be called a death wish.

Ball liked to raise garden vegetables, to read and quote Kipling, to play the violin. Never very close to his older squadron mates, he lived alone in a tent near his plane, where he could practice his music without disturbing others, and where he could scramble quickly if a Hun came over.

He flew with passion, munching a piece of cake, never wearing helmet and goggles because he liked the wind in his hair. Spotting an enemy plane, he'd head straight at it, odds be damned. He'd get very close—he was a bad shot—and then cut loose. He liked head-on passes, boring straight at a German until the enemy swerved and exposed a flank or a belly.

The enemy always did swerve from Ball. Perhaps they sensed that deliberate collision was a real threat. My squadron felt the same when Japanese pilots made head-on passes. A friend of mine, nicknamed "Judge," met such an attack from a "Tony," a Kawasaki Ki-61. They hurtled at each other, both blazing away, and when Judge had had enough and hit his stick forward, the Tony dove too, trying to hit him. They missed each other, but the leading edge of Judge's wing was torn up by ejected Japanese cannon shells.

Ball would deliberately let a German slide onto his tail, ready to open fire. At exactly the right moment, Ball would slap his stick forward, just as Judge did, and his plane would simply disappear. And as the enemy craned around to find him, Ball would zoom up from directly underneath, ready to blast that unguarded belly.

Once, chasing two Albatroses, Ball ran out of ammunition but harried them all the way back to their base nonetheless, trying to get close enough for a shot with his revolver. When they landed, he dropped a signed note challenging them to a duel.

He showed up for it the next day. The Germans were already circling, so he

Albert Ball was the first British flyer to become a popular hero. A Nieuport 17 with a wing-mounted Lewis suited his favorite tactic, shooting up through an enemy plane's belly, and he would employ it again with the S.E. 5a, his last plane. To the end, Ball put sheer daring and lone acts of bravery before tactics—habits that put him increasingly at risk as German (and British) formation flying improved.

43

bored straight in—and got trapped by three more Albatroses. He fought them all—one against five—until again his ammo was gone. Then he dove, pulled up, stalled, and spun. The Germans thought they had him. They still thought so when he broke the spin and landed in a meadow. Two landed beside him and started running toward him to take the great ace prisoner, for he was slumped in his cockpit, his propeller still idly turning.

And then, as the two Germans neared him, Ball suddenly came to life and crammed open his throttle. His S.E. 5 bounced into the air, whipped over the trees, and got him home unscathed.

Albert Ball hated killing, but knocked 44 enemy planes out of the sky. Then, on a May day in 1917, he simply disappeared. Tackling an Albatros in a wild dogfight, he was seen vanishing into a cloud bank. He never came out. The German press claimed Richthofen shot him down, but Richthofen didn't fly that day. No one knows what happened to Albert Ball, except that he found the death he had seemed so often to seek.

Ball was deeply mourned in the close-knit RFC. He left many young pilots inspired by his aggressiveness, and a good many of them followed him to the grave, for without restraint, such recklessness aims you straight at your headstone. James McCudden, who had never in his life charged headlong into combat, thought that A. P. Rhys-Davids would be the next great British ace. This delightfully modest and charming Etonian was racking up a good score against some elite German flyers. But he flew exactly like Ball, and in October 1917, he failed to return from a mission.

Instead, a close friend of McCudden became the next great RFC fighter pilot and the greatest British ace of the war. Edward Mannock learned combat tactics under McCudden, emulating his deliberate, systematic approach to air combat. But he got off to a very slow start.

A tall, saturnine Irishman, Mannock was no white-flanneled sporting Etonian, but a self-taught, disenchanted odd-jobber, considered politically radical because he espoused the underdog in general and the Labour Party in particular. He won no popularity contests with squadron mates. He was 29 years old and had a bad eye when he applied for flight training. He had trouble in flying school—sloppy landings, shaky formation work—and proved to be a lousy shot. It's a wonder the RFC took him in.

Tossed into a weary combat squadron, he worked desperately on his

Edward "Mick" Mannock fought the Germans with unwavering hatred. The writer Quentin Reynolds reports that when Mannock returned to base after shooting down a German plane, he'd say "Sizzle sizzle sizzle...I sent one to hell in flames today." Unlike Ball, Mannock tempered his ferocity with a strong sense of group tactics and had no equal among RFC officers as a teacher of new pilots.

weaknesses for two months and gained only a reputation for cowardice. His friend McCudden, watching from another squadron, knew that Mannock was trying to keep out of trouble until he could cope with it, and kept his fingers crossed for him.

In May 1917, a month after joining his squadron, Mannock managed to shoot down an observation balloon—no mean feat, incidentally; the Germans generally placed deadly antiaircraft batteries on the ground below. Although a balloon counted as a victory, Mannock's squadron mates paid no attention. Mannock kept to himself, flew constantly, and worked on gunnery, learning to compensate for his fluky eye.

And in two days in early July, he shot down two planes, then kept scoring again and again. By the end of that momentous month, the coward of the squadron had been

When S.E. 5s and S.E. 5as reached the front in April 1917, the RFC regained the upper hand over the German Albatros. The S.E. 5 was Britain's first tractor biplane fighter to use a water-cooled V-8 engine rather than a rotary, and its tremendous power and stability pleased Mannock, McCudden, Ball, and the other leading aces who flew it.

awarded a Military Cross, promoted, made a flight leader. Perhaps because of his own early troubles, Mannock liked to take new pilots with him, shepherding them carefully through their first missions. Often he'd hit an enemy plane, then swing away to let a novice blast it. Back on the ground, he'd say that he'd missed and credit the youngster with the victory. At briefings, he used his Irish eloquence to whip up eagerness for combat.

To Mick Mannock, the "German vermin," as he called them, embodied all that he hated—imperialism, arrogance, injustice, cruelty. Once, visiting another RFC squadron, Mannock tentatively joined in the usual evening revelry; but when a toast was drunk to Richthofen as a worthy enemy, Mick sat on his hands. "I won't lift a glass to that son of a bitch," he said.

He was surely their nemesis in the air: always above them, always cool-headed, he held off until exactly the right time, then killed swiftly and surely—often with a deflection burst, which he came to master. He shot down so many he lost count, even lost interest in the count, not bothering to confirm many of the planes he downed.

Mannock hated the idea of burning and carried a pistol when he flew. If he flamed, he said, he'd use it on himself. Exactly a year after he first started to score, his S.E. 5 was hit at low altitude, presumably by rifle fire from the trenches. He crashed in flames.

Maybe he used his pistol, but there wasn't much time. No one knows.

THE STORKS

The Royal Flying Corps contained a handful of especially famous squadrons, brilliant with stars: No. 56, where Ball flew his last missions and where McCudden later commanded a patrol; No. 40, where Mannock was first assigned; No. 74, the "Tiger" squadron, where he did much of his work. There were others, too, but none were intended as elite outfits. The RFC did not officially recognize aces, and the British press was slow to appreciate their news value.

But the French caught on quickly to the publicity value of air aces. Building elite squadrons, officers scouted for talent like American football coaches. Pierre Marinovitch was one find; only 20 when the war ended, he had three more victories than he did years. Jean-Pierre Bourjade, a student priest, went on after the war to tend lepers in the South Pacific. Hard-drinking Jean Navarre, one of the first Frenchmen to down a German, tore through the fleshpots of Paris as recklessly as through the skies, flew with a lady's stocking for a helmet, once carried a butcher's knife aloft in hopes of stabbing a zeppelin.

Most famous of all were the aces of a group known as *Les Cigognes*, "the Storks," from the insignia they painted on their planes. Originally a single squadron, Escadrille Nieuport No. 3, commanded by the brilliant Felix Brocard, the Storks were reorganized in October 1916 as a *groupe de chasse* with four squadrons of hand-picked pilots. Other escadrilles—*des Sportifs, les Coqs*—racked up impressive scores. But the Storks were the standard by which the rest were judged. They were the crème de la crème.

Georges Marie Ludovic Jules Guynemer joined Brocard's Escadrille No. 3 in June 1915. All five names belonged to one small, tubercular youth with wistful, dark eyes—the very antithesis of what most people think of as a fighter pilot. No one in his squadron believed that they had a hero in their midst. Guynemer's old and honored

Facing The Morane-Saulnier firm had given Roland Garros his first fighter and Anthony Fokker the design for his. Later Morane-Saulnier fighters were not as successful. Introduced in late 1917, the M-S A1 parasol monoplane looked promising. Its lines were clean, it boasted a Gnome Monosoupape 150-horsepower engine, and it was said to fly at 138 miles per hour. But French military officials couldn't shed lingering doubts about monoplanes' structural soundness. After two months at the front, the A1 was relegated to training.

family had helped persuade the military to overlook his health and accept him, and he'd charmed his way into flight training. Here he was, a corporal pilot—all 100 pounds of him. In his fighter, he was 100 pounds of wildcat. He'd approach a German plane tentatively, firing a brief burst to see what his enemy would do. It was as though he were reluctant to start the killing.

Once his victim reacted, the frail Frenchman was on him like a leech, following every twist, every frantic sideslip, every half roll and wingover and desperate dive. "I try anything I can," wrote Germany's great Ernst Udet, recalling an eight-minute dogfight with Guynemer, "but with lightning speed he anticipates all my moves and reacts at once. Slowly I realize his superiority." Somehow Udet survived; either Guynemer ran out of ammo, or (in another version of the story) he noticed that Udet's guns had jammed and gallantly let the German out of his clutches.

A British pilot who tried a little practice combat with Guynemer reported much the same feeling: "Nothing I could do would shift that grim-looking French scout off my tail."

I know that feeling too. In World War II, my squadron used to send a flight of P-39s to escort Australian Boomerangs, little ground-spotting and strafing planes. They were right on the deck, and we were slightly higher to chase away Zeroes and strafe any targets they marked with tracers. Flying home through the mountain passes, they'd "attack" us. These Aussies were all would-be fighter pilots, bored with their job (which was very dangerous), and they'd swarm all over our Airacobras. We were too low to dive away, and the damned little "Boomers," designed almost literally to twist through a rain forest, would slide into our hip pocket and stay there. "Ba-ba-ba-ba-ba-ba!" they'd shout in our earphones as they swung their gun sights on us. "Gotcha, Yank!" And so they had.

Guynemer flew every mission there was time for. He'd get sick, then bounce back. The press idolized him. He was given special-model Spads, one with a 37 mm cannon firing through the propeller shaft. His awed squadron mates noted that as he climbed into his cockpit his eyes would burn with purpose. He was like an executioner readying the guillotine.

He'd take on anything, any odds. Twice he shot down three planes in one day. On May 25, 1917, he got four. He was wounded eight times, crash-landed seven times, kept flying, though the brass begged him to rest.

Death wish? Guynemer as much as admitted it. "What new decoration can

Above Like Albert Ball, Georges Guynemer excelled at taking on the enemy alone. But where Ball put audacity before everything, Guynemer meticulously cultivated flying skills and was widely renowned for the finesse with which he flew his Nieuports and Spads.

Facing On July 19, 1915, Guynemer achieved his first victory, piloting a two-seater Parasol, a precursor of the Morane-Saulnier A1. He positioned the plane skillfully enough behind the enemy Aviatik that it took his observer-gunner only three minutes to send it down in flames. At the time, bringing down an enemy was rare enough that Guynemer received a medal for the feat.

Georges Guynemer and the rest of the Storks began their great period in Nieuports, then switched to the new Spad VII in the fall of 1916. Like the Royal Aircraft Factory's S.E. 5, the Spad broke new ground by using the Hispano-Suiza 150-horsepower water-cooled V-8 rather than a rotary. And like the S.E. 5, the Spad sacrificed a measure of maneuverability for increases in speed, rate of climb, and flight ceiling.

you possibly be looking for?" asked an adoring woman when he was in Paris conferring with the Spad people. "The wooden cross," he answered.

As it happened, Guynemer got nothing so simple. When he vanished in a dogfight in September 1917, no one ever found his body. The Germans claimed that his remains fell behind their lines and were obliterated during a British bombardment. But his memorial is graven in stone in the Panthéon of Paris with grandiose words about "indomitable tenacity of purpose," "ferocious verve," and "sublime gallantry."

A more touching memorial is the legend among French children that Georges flew so high he couldn't return to earth. He is still up there, still flying.

Guynemer's ferocity recalls the RFC's Albert Ball. René Fonck, France's top-scoring ace, was more like McCudden and Mannock. Fonck was a natural, a faultless pilot. He set about shooting down Germans with the fastidiousness of a surgeon diagnosing the situation and deftly excising the tumor.

He looked fastidious. Photographs always show Fonck nattily uniformed, kepi only slightly tilted above that fetching little wisp of a mustache. He resembled Max Immelman, and like him was ascetic in many ways, never drinking or indiscreetly womanizing. He tended to be terse, private, almost sullen, never joining the excited

chatter, complete with hand gestures, that all fighter pilots indulge in after a hairy mission. Instead, he took a nap.

No one much liked Fonck, and he diminished his popularity even more by boasting incessantly of his spectacular victories. Back before the days of gun cameras, a pilot who thought he'd clobbered an enemy plane would state his claim, then hope for confirmation from someone else in the air or on the ground. If a claim wasn't confirmed, the approved reaction was a Gallic shrug, a toast to the squadron's other victories, and a vow to drop the next enemy right on General Joffre's dinner table.

Unlike Mick Mannock, who often neglected to claim his victories, Fonck made claims all the time. He was set on being a glorious hero of France, whereas most other pilots didn't give a damn for that sort of thing.

It seemed that whenever Fonck flew alone, he'd return with some unbelievable tale of triumph. The rest of the Storks would listen in stony silence. Fonck himself firmly believed his claims and kept his own score, which added up to about 50 more victories than the 75 the government recognized.

Yet some of his farfetched tales proved to be true. On May 9, 1918, he claimed six German planes. Three of them fell in 45 seconds of combat, three more a few hours later. All were confirmed. And on August 14, he met an enemy formation of three planes and downed them all in ten seconds. They were easy to confirm, as they all hit the ground together within a few yards of each other.

René Fonck became the Allied Ace of Aces and France's top scorer because of his passion for every aspect of his craft, from the flying habits of his enemies to the condition of his ammunition. For a year, Fonck was a reconnaissance pilot, flying twin-engine Caudrons. Somehow he managed to bring down an Albatros D III from one of these hopelessly outmoded planes. To his delight, he joined a *groupe de chasse* in April 1917 and found himself at the controls of a Spad VII. Within a month, he'd brought down four Germans.

Right The Fokker D VIII (shown in replica) was Tony Fokker's last fighter for the Imperial German Air Service. Those who flew it found it extremely fast and agile. Its single wing, however, was not equal to the stresses of the high-speed dives and climbs of combat with Spads and S.E. 5s.

Facing Some of France's Spad VIIs bore the profile of a Sioux warrior on their fuselages. This was the insignia of the Lafayette Escadrille, a small group of Americans who were formally organized as a French fighter squadron in April 1916. One of their number, Kiffin Rockwell, opened the squadron's score in a spectacular way on May 16, bringing down an enemy with his first burst of fire on his first combat flight.

Amazingly, Fonck lived through the war. Nine years after the Armistice, he went after the $25,000 Orteig Prize for the first nonstop flight between Paris and New York. In his big Sikorsky trimotor he began his takeoff from Roosevelt Field, Long Island. But the huge load of fuel, too heavy for the landing gear, caused the plane to collapse. Instantly it flashed into an inferno of flame. And that was the end of René Fonck's dream of *la gloire*. He survived the crash, but must have been outraged that the glory went to a mere American, an air mail pilot, too young for the Great War.

The Storks were to produce another Orteig Prize contender, Charles Nungesser, a much earthier character than the fragile, ferocious Guynemer and the impeccable, unpopular Fonck. Although he had prewar flying experience, Nungesser was deemed too young for the air service, so he joined the cavalry. When it proved distressingly outmoded, he, like many other troopers, wangled a transfer.

He'd already shown himself a magnet for strange adventures. In the summer of 1914, as his cavalry regiment was retreating on its practically useless horses before the overwhelming German advance, young Charles led a patrol through enemy lines, ambushed and captured a German military car, and raced it back to his lines through a hail of rifle fire from both sides.

As a reconnaissance pilot, Nungesser constantly used his clumsy Voisin—armament, one rifle—as a fighter. His ground crew, sick of continually mending it, were happy to see him assigned to Nieuports. Stationed at Nancy, he buzzed the town so

Right An airplane seemed to obey Charles Nungesser's thoughts, not the controls, remarked James McConnell of the Lafayette Escadrille. McConnell had many opportunities to witness Nungesser's skill; for a month in 1916, the French ace shared combat patrols and nightlife with the American volunteers at their base near Luxeuil.

Facing Nungesser's flying skills were well-served by Gustave Delage's series of rotary-engine Nieuport biplanes. The Type 11 (Bébé) helped end the *Eindecker* menace; the Type 17 shown here was a principal opponent of the Albatros; and the Type 23 and Type 27 were flown by leading French pilots until the war's end. Their nimble handling was due in part to Delage's "sesquiplane" formula: a full upper wing and a much narrower, shorter lower wing. Nungesser adorned each of his Nieuports with an insignia of his own devising—two candles, a coffin, and a skull and crossbones, enclosed in a black heart.

outrageously that the mayor complained to Nungesser's C.O., who hauled him on the carpet and told him he should save his skills for the Germans. So Nungesser whipped over to a German air base and put on another show of low-level acrobatics, then returned to his base, where he was confined to quarters for eight days.

When this irrepressible young man wasn't in trouble with the brass, he was either surrounding himself with the ladies of Nancy, shooting down Huns, or recovering from various injuries. Handsome and likable, Charles Nungesser rolled up an impressive score, survived the war, and in May 1927, 12 days before Lindbergh's flight, set out for New York in a specially built white biplane, *l'Oiseau Blanc*.

The White Bird never arrived. Some people believe it crashed in the Maine woods; others say it was ditched near the French coast. With it was lost a remarkable flyer who had begun his career in the days of lone wolves and daredevils and somehow hung on long enough to benefit from the teamwork and formations that prevailed at the war's end.

RISE AND FALL OF THE FLYING CIRCUS

The dogfights of World War I raged on drawing boards as well as in the clouds. As a bright young American Army pilot, Major Hap Arnold noted, "The types changed so fast that the best plane on the line one day might very well be called obsolete the next."

Imperial Germany challenged French and British engineers with several strong designs in 1915 and 1916, and again with the Fokker D VII at the end of the war. In the fall of 1918, the D VII was the acknowledged champion of the skies, even better than the superb new Spad XIII, the legendary Sopwith Camel, and the S.E. 5.

Fortunately for Allied airmen, not that many Fokkers reached the front before the Armistice. But German pilots fought vigorously to the end, driving themselves toward the standard set by their idol—Manfred von Richthofen.

Enough has been written about this extraordinary fighter to stock a country library. Still, a few points are worth reconsidering. For one, Richthofen (like more than one of his Allied opponents) wasn't a natural flyer. Even today, fumbling students can be cheered by the knowledge that the matchless Red Baron ran into a heap of trouble as he learned his trade.

He came to the flying service in a roundabout way. Born in Breslau of a wealthy family, he hunted a great deal as a lad and became a splendid shot. Two years before the war, he joined a crack cavalry regiment. When war erupted, he and his whole regiment discovered that all the cavalry outfits in the world, even the First Uhlans, weren't good enough for modern warfare.

Relegated to supply services, the troopers idled restlessly in the rear lines. In the spring of 1915, 22-year-old Richthofen, never lacking in self-assurance, applied to his divisional commander for a transfer to the flying service. He let his Prussian hauteur spill over in an attached note: "My dear Excellency: I have not gone to war to collect cheese and eggs, but for another purpose."

Richthofen's plea was honored. Off he went to a training field, then to the

Above After the deaths of Max Immelman and Oswald Boelcke, Baron Manfred von Richthofen became Germany's leading fighter pilot. His *jasta*, staffed with aces like Werner Voss and Ernst Udet, was the most-feared German flying unit on the Western Front.

Facing The Fokker Dr I *Dreidecker*, which became the trademark of Baron von Richthofen and his "Flying Circus," was rapidly designed and produced in 1917 as an answer to Herbert Smith's Sopwith Triplane. Like the Triplane, the Dr I turned and twisted brilliantly in close dogfights—the combat situation for which it was specifically designed.

Russian Front as an observer, where he soon persuaded his pilot to give him flying lessons.

Richthofen hadn't a clue about the mechanics of a plane. Horses he understood; engines, no. And he lacked a feel for the air. The result was that it took him longer to solo than it did me, 27 years later, and that's saying a lot. My old log shows that I made 16 dual flights before going up alone. Richthofen flew dual 25 times before his instructor turned him loose. Then he smashed up on landing.

He'd have washed out of my primary training school. But in 1915, no one gave you a check ride, and if you were a proud young fire-eater with a Junker's social clout, you simply stared contemptuously at the nay-sayers and worked out your problems by yourself. Manfred's greatest Christmas present that year was to qualify at last as a pilot.

He flew two-seaters over the Eastern and Western Fronts, and shot down two planes—unconfirmed kills, which fell behind enemy lines. Ever an enthusiast for blood sports, he felt a dark joy in killing people, as though they were big game, and in Russia's uncontested skies, he bombed and strafed to his satisfaction.

Richthofen's hunting instincts impressed the great Oswald Boelcke when they met by chance. Assigned to Boelcke's *jasta* as a fighter pilot, he and the other "cubs" learned how to land the Halberstadt, then the Albatros, without cracking it up; how to take care of a machine gun, strip it, and sight it in; how to make a quick identification of enemy planes; how to plan the attack, close in, aim, fire, and break away cleanly.

When the cubs began flying patrols, Richthofen began scoring. On a September morning in 1916, the *jasta* met a flight of British F.E. 2s and swarmed in. Richthofen swung past one unsuccessfully, then returned, almost colliding as he opened fire. Even then, the British gunner nearly got him before the Fee went down, diving. It pulled up and thumped to a landing within the German lines, and, bursting with excitement, Richthofen all but crash-landed nearby. Running over, he found the gunner dead, the pilot dying. And he exulted.

The baron's eagerness almost lost him that victory. In the 79 that followed, as he became the world's undisputed top gun, he developed a cool, unfaltering technique. He would pick out his prey, study the odds, stalk, attack, and kill. His triumphs came fast. In the month of April 1917—"bloody April" to the Allies—he downed 21 planes, an average of one for every day he flew. He quickly rose to lead a flight, then his own *jasta*.

Occasionally his claims inspired a few whispered doubts within his flying circus. When they'd all shared a kill, he'd instinctively claim it for himself. He was no

For a year in 1916 and 1917, twin Spandau machine guns gave German fighter pilots a decided advantage in firepower. By the time the Fokker Dr I appeared, however, twin guns were being mounted on the Allies' new Spads, Sopwiths, and S.E. 5s. More seriously, these planes could outrun the Fokker, making it very difficult for *Dreidecker* pilots to initiate or break off a combat.

generous-hearted Mick Mannock. But he was no outrageous René Fonck either. His colleagues knew that when the Red Baron shot at something he was sure to hit it, so they accepted his claims with, perhaps, a wink and a shrug, but no kicks.

He never aimed just at the plane. He sighted on the man. If his target was a two-seater, he first fired at the observer-gunner, then the pilot. He carefully followed this procedure. To Richthofen, a kill was a real kill. Once the enemy went down, Richthofen would, if possible, visit the wreckage and pick up a souvenir. He was always a trophy hunter. Perhaps nothing brings the reality of war so clearly into focus as the baron's interest in his kills. If this handsome, well-brought-up young man seems to us moderns inordinately bloodthirsty, we are forgetting what a true warrior is all about. Not Rambo. The real thing is Richthofen.

He became a not-so-secret weapon. As his score mounted, he bore much of his nation's morale on his young shoulders. By the time he was killed, in April 1918, his very presence had raised the effectiveness of all German flyers. He had, moreover, influenced the design of two Fokker fighters, the notorious triplane and the superb D VII (which he never flew in action).

Instead, he was flying his trademark red Fokker Dr I that final Sunday. Another German flight had spotted a pair of enemy observation planes and attacked. A squadron of Sopwith Camels came to rescue the two-seaters. Richthofen's patrol saw

In his autobiography, Anthony Fokker wrote succinctly of his triplane's strengths and weaknesses. Allied pilots, he said, "never had an opportunity to realize how slow the triplane was because of the way it climbed, flipped, and stunted....Sometimes even German airmen were unaware of its limitations, the triplane responded so immediately to the demands of the fight when those demands became imperative."

Despite his successes with the Fokker Dr I, Richthofen kept pushing for a better plane. His favorite airplane maker, Tony Fokker, had lost the favor of the German aerial command, but with Richthofen's backing, Fokker managed to enter a prototype of the D VII in a design competition in January 1918. It won hands down, and after it reached combat in late April, pilots on both sides came to regard it as the war's best fighter.

the whirling mêlée and joined the fun.

One flight of Camels was led by a young Canadian, Captain Roy Brown. This was his 18th month of steady combat, and he was a cagy, cool-headed veteran with a dozen planes to his credit. He was also tired beyond belief and developing stomach ulcers. On this day he was trying to keep an eye on his newest replacement, a friend from Edmonton named Wilfred May.

Brown saw May attack a Fokker, then dive out of the tangle with another triplane, a bright red one, on his tail. Brown dove after them. "Wop" May twisted and skidded to throw off the triplane, but it hung on grimly, its twin Spandaus hammering away whenever the gun sight swung across him.

The German pilot, intent on a sure kill, never saw Roy Brown slip behind him and snuggle in close. Brown kicked his Camel straight, centered his sights and fired. The triplane's pilot wheeled around in his cockpit and stared for a moment at the Sopwith behind him as though he couldn't believe what was happening. Then he sagged forward, and his plane slid away and down. It landed by itself beside some Australian troops. Searching the dead pilot for identification, the soldiers were astonished to discover he was Baron von Richthofen.

The Australians put on a full-dress military funeral for the Red Baron, a strangely chivalric ritual with floral tributes from most of the British squadrons which had suffered from the German's skill. Afterward, a Camel buzzed the baron's home base and dropped a canister with a photograph of the funeral and a note:

To the German Flying Corps

Rittmeister Baron Manfred von Richthofen was killed in aerial combat on
April 21, 1918. He has been buried with all due military honours.

From the British Royal Air Force

The end of the baron marked the beginning of a new kind of aerial warfare. The greatest ace of all had been downed not by some heroic aerial duellist, but by a disciplined, well-trained fighter pilot just doing his job. The circus-red triplane, a symbol that inspired Germans and disturbed the sleep of Allied pilots, had been neatly trapped by a workaday Sopwith Camel. Things were changing.

Two days after a postmortem confirmed his incredible victory, Brown underwent emergency surgery for his ulcers, then was invalided back to England for the remainder of the war. His friend May didn't have a clue that his name would ever be remembered. He'd done what Brown had told him: dive away if you got in trouble. And suddenly he was caught in a blaze of notoriety. He recovered from it sufficiently to shoot down 13 planes and win a DFC.

The Canadians had no shortage of notable aces. Their best was Billy Bishop. He hailed from Owen Sound on Georgian Bay, had ridden horses and shot rifles for as long as he could remember, and had been at the Royal Military College at Kingston, Canada's West Point, when war broke out. Like so many fighter pilots back then, Bishop began his career in a cavalry outfit, then, disillusioned, transferred to the RFC as a gunner-observer. He applied for pilot training, was accepted, and joined a squadron in 1917, a lively, handsome lieutenant, eager for action.

He flew well, but despite being a crack shot with a rifle, found it hard at first to score hits with a machine gun fixed on the nose of a plane. One story has it that he practiced on empty tin cans, tossing them from his plane and firing at them as they tumbled down. Once he began to hit Germans, he hit often. In six weeks, he shot down 20 planes and made captain.

A bullet grazed Richthofen's skull in a dogfight on July 6, 1917. For a few moments, he was blinded and paralyzed; his plane spun out of control. Somehow he managed to land behind German lines before blacking out. Returning to the air the next month, he fought on with his usual deadly efficiency. But those who knew the baron well detected a change in his spirit—as if he had realized that even he could be killed in the sport he had mastered.

Above German aces like Ernst Udet lived to benefit from Richthofen's support of the remarkable Fokker D VII. While the last German offensives on the ground were collapsing, Udet and his colleagues harried Allied pilots to the end; in August 1918 alone, the *jastas* supplied with D VIIs brought down 565 Allied planes.

Right Flying mostly in Nieuports, Canadian Billy Bishop shot down 72 enemy planes in less than two years on the Western Front. Eddie Rickenbacker, the top American ace, considered him the war's finest— and most fearless—fighter pilot.

Facing The Siemens Schuckert D III was a rotary-powered German fighter of 1918. With an excellent climbing rate and good maneuverability, it typified fighter design in the war's last year.

Bishop was a daredevil. On one especially busy day, he took on a total of 23 enemy planes. And a lone early-morning strafing attack on a German airfield wiped out a bunch of planes, three of them in the air, and won him a Victoria Cross. Finally, during his last 12 days at the front, he shot down 25 German planes. Amazingly, he lived through the first war and served his country as an air marshal in the next.

On the German side, a small, cocky, likable young pilot in the Richthofen fighter group took the lead among aces. Ernst Udet, who had survived a run-in with Georges Guynemer, got through the war with 62 victories. He became famous afterward on flying tours of Argentina, Africa, Greenland, and the United States, and wrote *Mein Fliegerlieben*, translated as *Ace of the Iron Cross*. The book is rich in details about flying which still had meaning for a pilot of my era. He notes, for example, that on cold winter days the open cockpit can be pleasurable "if one wraps up well and butters the face." I learned to fly in an open cockpit in February, but never heard of buttering the face.

Udet tells how he would block the sun with his thumb, the better to search the sky. I was taught to do that too. I still did it years later when I used to fly a little rented Cessna for fun.

And in his first confrontation with an enemy plane, he admits, he simply came apart. The Frenchmen, flying a Caudron, came straight at him until even the features of the observer in the front seat were clear. "With his square goggles, he looked like a giant, malevolent insect coming toward me to kill. The moment has come when I must fire. But I can't..."

For a new pilot in my day, such a classic case of "buck fever" would have been

Formed in 1916, the Lafayette Escadrille brought together a group of Americans scattered through the French air force, the Foreign Legion, and the American Ambulance Field Service. The French lodged, fed, and supplied their American associates so well that James McConnell, an original member, wondered at first whether he "was a summer resorter or a soldier...then I recalled the ancient custom of giving a man selected for the sacrifice a royal time of it before the appointed day." Escadrille members depicted in the photograph are (left to right) William Thaw, Robert Soubiran, Ray C. Bridgeman, Chris Ford, and DeFreest Larner. Thaw was another founding member, and later commanded the 103rd Aerial Squadron.

fatal. Udet got away with a light wound and a bullet-riddled plane. And as he scurried shamefully home, he had "only one thought: 'Thank God, no one saw this!'" That feeling I can understand. Flying so often alone, World War I pilots were spared some embarrassing moments. A generation later, when I erred on my early missions (and some later ones), I always had witnesses, at least one, usually three, sometimes fifteen. Formation flying was the only way to go in World War II, and every man's failures were noted with thin-lipped displeasure by his element leader, the rest of his flight, frequently his whole squadron.

Udet calls Richthofen, his group commander, "the least complicated man I ever knew. Entirely Prussian and the greatest of soldiers." He seems to have gotten along all right with Hermann Göring, who took over the Richthofen fighter group "because," said Udet, "he is regarded as the foremost air strategist of the Army." Clearly, Udet would have preferred the command for himself or at least another member of

Richthofen's *jasta*.

Despite his Prussian nature, Richthofen had run his command rather loosely, setting an example for his pilots to emulate, giving them free rein not to do so, never bothering them with military folderol. He turned them into an aerial version of Lord Nelson's "band of brothers": an efficient—and happy—command.

Göring came from outside the fraternity and ran it with a rigidity no one was accustomed to. He was a good pilot and shot down 22 planes, but unlike his predecessor, he didn't live for piling up victories. Instead, he sought always to feed his vanity, which was considerable even then. The best way to gain renown, he found, was through administration.

So Göring flew his desk more than his all-white Fokker. He'd blister his men for straying from the book, then switch on his massive charm to ease the tension. After the war, he made friends with another veteran who used the same technique—an ex-corporal named Adolph Hitler. In Hitler's Germany, Göring commanded the Luftwaffe. His old squadron mate, Ernst Udet, also attained high rank, only to be betrayed by Göring, who blamed him for the Luftwaffe's failures. Loving his country but despising the Nazis who ran it, Udet committed suicide.

Udet's book, a valuable record of German flying, stands out among flyers' memoirs. Other fine accounts came from the Allies, particularly the Americans. Many

When Raoul Lufbery took Douglas Campbell and Eddie Rickenbacker on their first combat patrol in 1918, he'd been flying in combat for three years. He led them over the German lines, but cannily steered clear of enemy planes. Back at the base, he asked what they'd observed. Campbell and Rickenbacker replied that they'd seen no planes, Allied or German. "Luf" informed them that ten Spads had flown within 500 yards of the Americans, and four German Albatroses were approaching from two miles away when he decided to turn for home with his trainees. "You must learn to look around a bit when you get in enemy lines," he concluded.

of the 49 adventurous young Yanks who served with the famed Lafayette Escadrille before their country entered the war wrote spirited letters or memoirs, and from these emerged a number of books.

As a boy, I buried myself in James Norman Hall's *High Adventure*, in *Falcons of France* by Hall and Charles Nordhoff, in *The Great Adventure* by Ted Parsons. These true accounts balanced the wild improbabilities of the pulp magazines. I know that most of the young men in my fighter squadron grew up reading the same things. We thought we had an idea of what we were getting into, and in a few ways we were right.

When the United States joined the war, these blooded veterans of the Lafayette Escadrille often failed to meet the bureaucratic standards of the American Aerial Service. Bill Thaw, the first American flyer to go into action, had a bad eye, bad hearing, and a bad knee. Raoul Lufbery, the Escadrille's top ace, was over the age limit. Only special waivers got them and many others into the 103rd and other new squadrons.

Joining the Americans was not what they expected. Despite congressional promises to darken the sky with planes, not a single American aircraft reached France during the war. So the Lafayette stars had to cool their heels, training the new American Air Service pilots in war-weary Spads and Nieuports that lacked machine guns.

Poor Raoul Lufbery, supremely good in the air and all but useless at administration, was assigned to a desk. Finally, he got into the 94th, which would become the famous "Hat-in-the-Ring" squadron, and for a month he led training patrols with the new pilots.

Then, in March 1918, American Expeditionary Force suppliers scrounged up enough machine guns for three planes, and "Luf" went back to building his score. He seemed happier, but he was a strange fellow, hard to know, completely uninterested in publicity. His colleagues recalled his fear of burning. If he should flame after being hit, he avowed, and couldn't blow out the fire by sideslipping, he'd rather die by jumping.

Under Luf's tutelage, Doug Campbell and Alan Winslow each bagged a German plane on a single day that March, the first victories for an American unit. No longer would the Yanks be called "impatient virgins." Two months later, Luf was hit by the rear gunner of a two-seater, and his Nieuport exploded in roaring flames. And he jumped. His body was found in a cottage garden in a little French village.

James Norman Hall joined the Americans, was made a combat instructor, then got back into the action and was shot down. Slightly wounded, he was taken prisoner. He lived to write those memoirs, and he teamed up with Nordhoff (another flyer) on the

unforgettable *Bounty* trilogy. One of his early flight students, and later the most famous protégé of Lufbery in the 94th Squadron, was a well-known race-car driver named Eddie Rickenbacker.

In his autobiography, Rickenbacker revealed that he had to conquer a tendency toward air sickness before he began clobbering Germans. His fifth score was almost his last. He dove after his victim, hit him, then hauled the stick back to face two other Albatroses: "A ripping, tearing crash shook the plane. The entire spread of linen over the right upper wing was stripped off..."

Spinning down, the American tried a burst of power and, perhaps because of torque, managed to level off. Losing altitude all the way home, he landed safely—at full throttle. He went on to become the leading American ace with 26 victories. Ever likable and tolerant, "Rick" recalls in his book one fellow pilot who reached the point where he simply refused to fly. He was scared and he admitted it freely. The man was

The United States promised to send thousands of planes to Europe in 1918. In fact, not one genuinely American fighter plane reached the front, and the first Aero Squadrons had to take whatever French and British manufacturers could spare. Eddie Rickenbacker's 94th "Hat-in-the-Ring" Squadron got the Nieuport 28, which the French government had rejected. The Americans quickly found out why: in a dive, as Rickenbacker later wrote, '28s "had a grim tendency to shed their wings." Rickenbacker himself nearly crashed when his Nieuport 28 lost the fabric on its upper wing, and several American pilots were killed in similar accidents.

Above Eddie Rickenbacker shot down 26 German planes in a remarkably short period—six months of active combat service. He was quickly promoted and proved to be a popular, effective squadron leader as well.

Facing The combat career of the Curtiss JN-4 Jenny was brief. Eight went to Mexico with General Pershing in 1916, and the four that managed to get near the fighting succumbed to engine troubles in the dust and heat. Reassigned to training, however, the slow and stable Jenny proved to be an ideal beginner's plane. The U.S. Army Service purchased thousands, and Jennys served at training schools and on mail routes well into the twenties.

transferred, and, says Rick, "None of us felt any rancor." That was true in my day. No pilot in my squadron ever used the word "coward." If someone chickened out, it was too bad. But it was also entirely understandable.

Sometimes a pilot became almost mad in his *lack* of fear. Such a man was Rickenbacker's colleague, Frank Luke. Raised in Arizona, Luke was a loner, unused to being noticed. He took on the hazardous job of blowing up observation balloons and became a terror to German artillery spotters and the pilots of their covering aircraft. Attacking in the evening, he would come in low, suddenly darting through the ring of deadly accurate ground fire that guarded the balloons. He'd flame a hydrogen gas bag and often down a patrolling Fokker with it.

Depressed by the loss of two of his few squadron friends, he slipped away from reality—and (without leave) from his base. And then one autumn evening, he slipped away for the last time. He passed through a storm of bullets to down three balloons. Badly hit, his plane a smoking sieve, he strafed a mass of enemy troops before crash-landing. As the German infantry came for him, he rested his bleeding body against a tree, fished out his big Colt and an extra clip, and shot 11 of them before they got him. Frank Luke won a posthumous Medal of Honor. He'd been in action exactly 17 days and scored 21 times.

His name lives in the United States, along with Rickenbacker's and that of their commanding general, Billy Mitchell. They remind us that in their brief blaze of fighting in 1918, American flyers began a tradition of bravery, skill, and ingenuity. Their deeds glowed in contrast to their country's braggadocio, production lapses, administrative blindness.

As peace returned to the world, these failings were forgotten and even the horror of the war's unspeakable slaughter dimmed somewhat. But the memory of those first fighter pilots, their legacy of strength and valor, have endured, inspiring flyers ever since in peace and war.

BETWEEN WARS

When American flyers came home from World War I, many weren't ready to give up the excitement of flying high-strung combat planes for the dull safety of peacetime life. But the military didn't have much for them to do at home. Those were more primitive times, when a mountainous national debt was unthinkable, and Congress reduced the Army Air Service from 200,000 men in 1918 to 10,000 in 1920.

The fighter pilots who stayed on found themselves patrolling the Pacific Northwest's forests to spot fires and the Mexican border to spot illegal immigrants. Some flew the "flaming coffin," the disappointing American-built D.H. 4; some risked their necks in the handsome but very dicey Thomas Morse Scout, powered by a rotary engine with a disconcerting habit of shutting off abruptly in flight. Most chugged around in the faithful old trainer, the Curtiss Jenny. If something went wrong with it, you could (so they say) mush it into the trees and climb down.

Some who didn't find a place in the peacetime Air Service became stunt flyers, often using surplus Jennys sold by the government at bargain prices. When a stuntman flew into a farmer's meadow near a little town, his plane might be the first the locals had ever seen. The career of more than one World War II fighter pilot must have been inspired in these out-of-the-way places as young boys watched the rolls and spins and dives of daredevils from the first air war.

Billy Mitchell, the outspoken, dynamic commander of AEF air squadrons in World War I and assistant chief of the Army Air Service from 1920 to 1925, tried harder than anyone to keep the nation convinced of aviation's importance. A disciple of Boom Trenchard, he looked enviously at Great Britain, where the Royal Flying Corps and the Royal Naval Air Service had been brought together as a fully independent service, the Royal Air Force, and he lobbied ferociously to get the same status for American flying forces.

No go, said wiser heads. Men like General John Pershing weren't convinced by what they'd seen in World War I that aviation could play a decisive role in future wars. Mitchell's criticism of Air Service policy would earn him nothing more than a court martial and the end of his military career in 1925.

Above Henry "Hap" Arnold became a military aviator in 1911 and was trained on a Wright military *Flyer* by the brothers themselves. When he retired from his post as the first commanding general of the United States Air Force in 1952, he had supervised the growth of the most powerful air force in history, guiding it to victory in the first war decided by air power. Friendly, energetic, and strong-willed, Arnold was known as a "superb fixer" with an instinct for getting the most from his colleagues—men like Ira Eaker, Pete Quesada, Carl Spaatz, and Jimmy Doolittle—and a flair for winning his way with Congress and the President.

Facing Wood, fabric, and wire, the materials which show so clearly in this Curtiss Jenny, were still what planes were made of as World War I ended. Only Germany's Junkers company had explored all-metal construction in the J 1 of 1915 and the D I and CL I of 1918.

Americans pioneered flight from ships, but the British were the first to put the new idea to military use. A Sopwith Pup landed on HMS *Furious* on August 2, 1917—the first shipboard landing since Eugene Ely's in 1911. And later that month, a Pup took off from HMS *Yarmouth* and knocked down a German Zeppelin along the Danish coast—the first aerial victory for a carrier-based fighter.

Even when the U.S. Air Force was finally established in 1947, it would not include Navy flyers. Stubborn as an army mule, the U.S. Navy balked at giving away its pet daughter in marriage. And no wonder—the Navy pilots of World War II counted some of the world's finest flyers among their ranks. Zinging off the decks of huge aircraft carriers in their Wildcats, Hellcats, and Corsairs, their Dauntlesses and Avengers, they did as much as anyone to awaken the Japanese from their dream of a Greater East Asia Co-Prosperity Sphere.

Their enthusiasm went all the way back to October 1910, when naval aviation got started. Picture the excitement of the Belmont aviation meet, held at the famous race track near New York. Among the fashionably dressed ladies and gentlemen marveling at the Wright and Curtiss planes was stiffly-uniformed Captain Washington Irving Chambers, Annapolis class of 1876. He was there at the Navy's command to find out all he could about airplanes. One question especially concerned him: could a plane fly from the deck of a ship?

One of Glenn Curtiss' test pilots, J.A.D. McCurdy of Canada, obviously thought so. He was already planning to take off from a German transatlantic liner, demonstrating a way to carry passengers' mail to shore. Chambers asked Wilbur Wright if he would take off from a warship. No way, said Wilbur. The next week, at an air show in Baltimore, Chambers tried another young Curtiss test pilot, Eugene Ely, whom he had met at Belmont. Sure, said Ely, he'd like to try it with his own plane—at no charge to the Navy.

Chambers and some equally fevered Navy friends lobbied the Navy Secretary, who balked at the cost of building a launch platform on a ship until a millionaire aviation fanatic named John Ryan contributed $1,000. Now they had to hurry; McCurdy had scheduled a flight for November 5. Bad weather forced him to postpone it until November 12, and on that day, as the plane warmed up, an oil can tumbled into the propeller and broke it.

On November 14, Gene Ely sat in his Curtiss pusher at the top of a sloping ramp built over the foredeck of the cruiser USS *Birmingham*, near Norfolk, Virginia. Only 57 feet of flight deck stretched before him. The plan was to take off into the wind while the vessel was under way, but squalls had forced the cruiser to anchor.

Birmingham's bow swung into the wind; Ely gunned his engine, signaled for release, trundled down the ramp—and disappeared under the bow. A spurt of spray rose and the hearts of the watchers sank. Then the plane wobbled into sight, low over the waves, heading for shore. It had brushed the water and cracked its propeller blades, but the pilot nursed it to a safe landing on solid ground. Eureka!

Now, how about landing on a ship? Chambers and company went to work again, this time in San Diego, and two months after his heart-stopping takeoff, Ely flew out to the anchored USS *Pennsylvania*, slid onto a 120-foot ramp, and stopped neatly when sandbagged ropes snagged the hooks he had affixed under his plane. After celebrating with the ship's captain, Ely took off from the platform—no sweat this time— and flew back to shore. And so, on January 18, 1911, U.S. Naval Aviation was born,

Eugene Ely had offered to make his pioneering flight from USS *Birmingham* at no charge to the Navy. His propeller was damaged as his Curtiss plane grazed the water, and when John Ryan, the millionaire who financed the building of the launch ramp, gave him the cash to repair it, Ely used it to buy a diamond for his wife Mabel. Glenn Curtiss, Ely's employer, was also well rewarded for the experiment. He demonstrated a floatplane for the Navy in January 1911 and delivered the first of a long line of Navy Curtiss floatplanes in July.

Overleaf Many pilots of the 1920s honed their skills flying Curtiss Jennys on new air mail routes. A Curtiss Jenny of the Army Air Service inaugurated regular air mail service in the United States on May 15, 1918, taking off from Washington for Philadelphia and New York. As the story goes, the pilot became lost over Maryland, cracked his propeller on landing, and quietly sent the first air mail bag on by train.

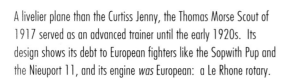

A livelier plane than the Curtiss Jenny, the Thomas Morse Scout of 1917 served as an advanced trainer until the early 1920s. Its design shows its debt to European fighters like the Sopwith Pup and the Nieuport 11, and its engine *was* European: a Le Rhone rotary.

and coming generations of carrier pilots would have Gene Ely to thank—often to curse—for their demanding profession.

The Navy's infant air arm, like the Army's, was raised in poverty. Even the outbreak of World War I in 1914 had little impact on our national budget. The fighting was 3,000 miles away, so why worry? When France appropriated seven million dollars for aviation, the native land of the Wright brothers grudgingly spared a measly $140,000.

As we entered the 1920s, airmen of both the Army and Navy needed all the friends at court they could muster. Once, before the war, the Navy's John Towers and the Army's Hap Arnold, close friends and fellow pilots, swapped uniforms as a gag at a formal function. That was probably the closest the two services ever came to forming a unified air force.

Vying for funds, Army and Navy flyers took separate paths. To gain publicity—and hopefully a congressional handout—Billy Mitchell and his Army Air Service pushed at the envelope of aircraft performance, pioneering new routes, setting distance and endurance records, competing in air races.

As they started going after records, Jimmy Doolittle came into his own. He was a rugged young Army lieutenant who had, to his disgust, spent the war years as an instructor. In 1922, he flew a D.H. 4 across the country within the span of a day. In

1924, he was chosen to test fly a Fokker and managed to pull nearly eight Gs coming out of a dive, thus discovering how the wing structure stood pressure (it failed) and how much a man could take (he blacked out).

A year later, Doolittle won the Schneider Trophy Race, an international event for seaplanes, clocking 232 miles per hour around a pylon-marked course on the Chesapeake Bay. The next day, he upped that world record by 10 miles per hour. His dainty little black and gold Curtiss R3C-2, the last biplane to win the trophy, was the prototype for Curtiss' Hawk series, the principal American pursuit planes of the twenties.

Jimmy went on testing himself and his various aircraft. Puzzling over the effect of negative Gs—pressure exerted on the top of a plane rather than the bottom—he pushed a Curtiss P-1 Hawk into a dive, then held the stick forward to complete the world's first outside loop. This time he "redded out"—blood rushed to his head, suffusing his eyes—but the Hawk held together. Few people ever did an outside loop again. Still, it was nice to know that you could.

This urge to experiment marked Doolittle's career. He was a scholar with a doctorate from MIT, and was largely responsible for the growth of instrument flight between the wars. He made the first blind flight—all on instruments—in 1929. Then, as an exciting vacation from his studies, he won the Bendix and Thompson trophies and set two more speed records, one for a transcontinental flight, in the early thirties.

Other Army pilots set records too. In 1923, Lieutenants Oakley Kelley and John Macready flew their big, awkward Fokker T-2 on the first nonstop flight across the country. Then came the World Cruisers of 1924. Four husky two-man biplanes, built

Above "I have never felt fear," said James Doolittle at the age of ninety. "I am single-minded. I think of only one thing at a time, and if I'm in a very tight spot indeed, I'm thinking about how to get out of that hot spot." That level-headedness made Doolittle as renowned as Lindbergh in the twenties and thirties, and pulled him through one of World War II's most daring aviation exploits—the bombing raid on Tokyo in 1942.

Left With fighters like the Curtiss P-1 Hawk of 1925, American military aviation began to catch up with the French and the British. The first Hawks were built around the Curtiss D-12 inline engine, which had speeded a Curtiss entry past French and British racers to win the Schneider Trophy in 1923.

by young Donald Douglas as Navy torpedo aircraft, set out from Seattle to be the first aerial circumnavigators. Two made it all the way, returning to Seattle five and a half months after leaving. The crews of all four planes were safe.

Congress had begun to believe in aviation's military value, and in 1926, the Army Air Service became the Army Air Corps—a more independent branch. To celebrate, five Loening amphibians took off on a goodwill flight to South America. One crashed in Argentina, but four finished safely, despite some hair-raising adventures. Among their pilots were Ira Eaker and Ennis Whitehead, who became leading Army Air Force generals in World War II. A few years later, Eaker and two more future Air Force greats, Tooey Spaatz and Pete Quesada, were among the crew that set a flight endurance record by refueling, air-to-air, 43 times. They had named their Fokker triplane *Question Mark* because they didn't know how long it would stay up. Answer: almost a week. Once the refueling hose pulled loose and Spaatz got drenched with gasoline. His friends stripped off his clothes to avoid high-octane inflammation, and stark naked in the icy air, Spaatz fed the hose back into the tank.

Plenty of Army pilots resigned to go barnstorming. Charles A. Lindbergh reversed the process. He quit an engineering course and learned to fly as a barnstormer. Then he joined Army aviation and graduated at the top of his class. By the time he set out for Paris in *Spirit of St. Louis*, he had racked up plenty of night flights on primitive instruments in lousy weather with overloaded planes. His engineering skills were sharper than ever. He took off from Long Island's Roosevelt Field with the attitude of a scientist demonstrating a known fact.

The press, frantically trying to glamorize this unknown, absorbed, very private man, hit on things like "Lucky Lindy" and "The Flyin' Fool"—ironic sobriquets for one of the most meticulous, mathematically thorough, and skillful pilots who ever lived.

Most headlines for record-setting went to the Army. But the Navy gained a few. A crew of seven naval aviators made the first transatlantic flight in 1919 in a big Curtiss flying boat, the NC-4. Admiral Richard E. Byrd also won the service plenty of coverage with his polar explorations. Mostly, though, Navy Air worked on innovative and often hair-raising flying techniques to demonstrate military uses for its spectacular and expensive aircraft carriers and dirigibles.

In the twenties and thirties, the world was in love with the dirigible. So huge they seemed to darken the sky, these great silver vessels—truly ships of the air— expressed perfectly man's ingenuity, his hopes and dreams. As a boy I watched, of

Charles Lindbergh's pioneering flights showed that with meticulous planning and the right equipment, long-distance flying could become a safe, routine occurrence. His keen eye and thorough nature were invaluable to Hap Arnold and the Army Air Force in 1939. On his return that year from a long stay in Europe, Lindbergh sat with Arnold in the bleachers during a baseball game at West Point and told him all he knew about the ominous capabilities of Hitler's Luftwaffe. Armed with Lindbergh's insights, Arnold pushed for planes that would match or surpass Germany's best.

course, when a dirigible flew overhead. Everybody watched. Entire cities would turn out onto the streets to stare at that massive, man-made, metallic cloud. I found something magically human about it. It passed slowly with a friendly, nonthreatening drone. And its landings, as seen in countless newsreels, had a gargantuan charm, the giant craft nuzzling ponderously at its mooring mast like a circus elephant snuffling for a peanut.

Shenandoah, Los Angeles, Akron, and Macon were our Navy's dirigibles. One by one, all but Los Angeles were lost in bad weather, and the Navy had to admit that these extravagant vessels (costing millions of dollars apiece) weren't suited to warfare. And when the German Hindenburg exploded and burned in 1937, right at that charming moment of mooring, all the dirigible's elephantine friendliness went up in her flames. That was the end of the love affair for me—and, it turned out, for the rest of the world as well.

But in their short life, dirigibles inspired one innovation that stirred the blood of all flight-happy lads in knickerbockers: the hook-on. The idea was to keep a few small fighters aboard an airship so they could be lowered and released to zoom off on protective missions. Returning, each fighter pilot would carefully snuggle under the mother ship's belly and latch on like a suckling piglet. Then the plane was hauled into the dirigible's innards, and the pilot would crawl out of his cockpit and presumably head for the bar. Curtiss built a special little fighter, the Sparrowhawk, which the dirigible carried like an airborne dinghy. I wanted to fly it.

Carriers were something else, and the prospect of landing on one in a rough

Boeing P-12 fighters were propelled by radial engines—one of the most important technological achievements in aviation in the twenties. A radial engine's ring of cylinders doesn't spin with the propeller, offering the advantage of air-cooling and easy access to each cylinder without the rotary's tremendous torque. Working with the Boeing Company, the Navy procured a series of radial-engine biplane fighters for carriers, where the maintenance demands of water-cooled engines could be troublesome. The fourth of the series, the F4B, caught the Army's attention, and its variant, the P-12, became the main Air Corps fighter of the early thirties.

One of the best-known biplanes in history, the de Havilland Tiger Moth was the principal basic trainer of the Royal Air Force for 15 years after its introduction in 1931. Most RAF and Commonwealth pilots of World War II began military flying in the versatile biplane. After the war, turning swords into ploughshares, Tiger Moths pioneered crop-dusting techniques. Surplus Tiger Moths—over 5,000 were built—also became prized possessions among private flyers worldwide.

Above Even as monoplanes were reaching fighter squadrons in the late thirties, the biplane remained the best trainer configuration. The Focke-Wulf Fw 44 was a primary trainer for the Luftwaffe.

Right and Far Right The Polikarpov Po-2 was the Soviet equivalent of the Tiger Moth. Over 20,000 of these planes were built between 1928 and 1952—more than any other Soviet aircraft in history. Used as a primary trainer in World War II, the Po-2 was also pressed into service as a reconnaissance plane and for night bombing raids. Some were even equipped with loudspeakers for propaganda missions.

Above While the Soviets were learning their trade in Po-2s and the British in Tiger Moths, American flyers trained on the forgiving and beautiful Boeing Stearman Kaydet. Lloyd Stearman designed the plane in 1934, and it soon won the Army Primary Trainer Competition. After Boeing bought his company, it continued to produce the aircraft with a variety of different engines through 1945; over 10,000 were built in all.

Right The Curtiss Sparrowhawk was designed as a carrier-based fighter. Proving too dangerous for carrier work, it was chosen for the Navy's plan to guard the nation's coasts with airships. Airships could survey much larger areas than ships at sea, and with a brace of Sparrowhawks making reconnaissance and defensive patrols, that area could be extended even farther. The "Men on the Flying Trapeze" insignia on the Sparrowhawk's fuselage perfectly expressed the skillful piloting required to dock the little plane on a moving airship.

Facing The Boeing F4B/P-12 was purchased in larger numbers than any other American fighter between the wars, and during its four years of production, it was continually improved. On the P-12E and F4B-3 of 1931, a semimonocoque fuselage and Townend cowling ring around the engine helped reduce drag, and more powerful versions of the superb Pratt & Whitney R-1340 radial engine increased the plane's top speed to 188 miles per hour.

sea at night was daunting even to an 11-year-old. I was about that age when my school class visited the brand-new *Lexington*. She and *Saratoga*, commissioned in 1927, were adapted from heavy cruisers. They were the longest, most powerful ships then afloat, carried up to 90 planes, and could launch and land them quickly. They pointed the way for the great ships that followed: *Ranger*, *Yorktown*, and *Enterprise*, built entirely as carriers.

Americans got the credit for the first shipboard landings and takeoffs, but British naval aviators were the first to test the carrier's military usefulness, flying Sopwiths from the deck of a converted cruiser, HMS *Furious*, in World War I. After the war, the U.S. Navy studied what the British had done and learned many useful lessons. The Japanese, too, liked the looks of HMS *Furious*: they launched *Hosho*, the first ship built specifically as a carrier, in 1922. William Jordan of the RFC, who'd become a Mitsubishi test pilot, made *Hosho*'s first carrier landings and takeoffs, flying a Mitsubishi Type 10 designed by Herbert Smith, who thought up many of Sopwith's great wartime planes.

Proving the wisdom of its separateness from the Army, the United States Navy Air established formidable training schools at Pensacola and other bases and produced extremely capable pilots, well versed in navigation and in flying a variety of aircraft types. The very best of these cadets went to the carriers to fly dive-bombers, torpedo-bombers, or fighters.

In the midthirties, Hollywood movies began to appear about naval flying—usually with Pat O'Brien in them—featuring fine camera shots of fat little Navy Grumman

Above Three of the United States' first four aircraft carriers are shown here patrolling the Pacific in the 1930s. USS *Ranger*, in the foreground, was the first American ship designed from the keel up as a carrier. A squadron of Grumman F3F-1s are spotted on her deck. USS *Lexington* and *Saratoga*, steaming ahead of her, were the largest military vessels of their time. *Lexington* was lost to Japanese dive-bombers on the second day of the Battle of the Coral Sea in 1942; *Saratoga* served through the war and met her end as a test vessel during the atomic bombing of Bikini in 1946.

Facing The Grumman FF-1's retractable wheels were a first among American military aircraft. The Navy contract for the FF-1 was also a first for Grumman, which continues to build a frontline Navy fighter even today—the F-14 Tomcat. The F2F and the F3F, larger, faster versions of the "Fifi," were the Navy's last biplane fighters.

F3F biplanes, wheels tucked up, forming a V of V's over a mighty carrier. Newsreels often showed an Army Air Service squadron of dainty Boeing P-26 "Peashooters"—all-metal monoplanes with their wheels in streamlined pants, all in a long, straight echelon. After many evenings of this, Americans would feel pretty comfortable about defense.

Our planes looked great on the screen, but they had never been tested in war. We knew that the Army pilots, white scarves whipping back from their open cockpits, cherished the tradition of achieving goals, and that the Navy flyers, peering from their canopies, had been gleaned from perhaps the world's most intensive and demanding training. Yet in 1933, when Germany's new *Führer* introduced the secretly trained Luftwaffe to the world, Pensacola trained only 30 Navy pilots. When Hitler sent the

Above The Hawker Demon, which the RAF flew from 1932 to 1939, was the first British two-seater fighter since the Bristol fighter of 1917. The Demon closely resembled Sydney Camm's most beautiful biplane fighter, the single-seat Hawker Fury. Both were built around the Rolls-Royce Kestrel V-12 engine, a forerunner of the great V-12s of the Hurricanes and Spitfires.

Right Aviators of the United States Marine Corps flew land-based variants of the Navy Boeings. The F4B-3 of 1932 (shown in replica) was the first of the F4B series to have a metal fuselage.

Above The U.S. Navy's first all-metal monoplane fighter, the Brewster F2A Buffalo, had a short, unhappy career. After beating out a prototype of the Grumman F4F Wildcat in Navy tests in 1937, the Buffalo was in turn outclassed by an improved F4F the next year, and the Navy quickly replaced it. Many were sold to Great Britain, the Netherlands, and Finland; in the Dutch East Indies, they quickly succumbed to vastly superior Mitsubishi A6M Zeroes. But Finnish pilots, exploiting the Buffalo's ruggedness and high roll rate, scored impressive victories over faster, nimbler Soviet opponents.

Left The ungainly appearance of the Polikarpov I-16 belies its place in aviation history. When the prototype appeared in 1933, its low-wing monoplane configuration and retractable wheels were well in advance of European and American designs. In the late thirties, facing German Heinkel He 51s in Spain and the first Japanese monoplanes in Manchuria, the I-16 proved itself a useful, capable fighter.

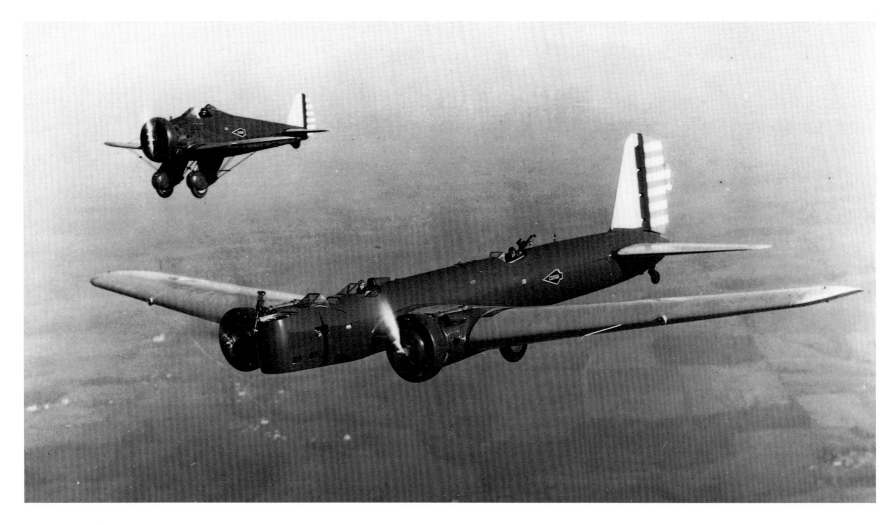

Above American fighter designs of the 1930s began to reflect a new mission: intercepting long-range bombers. Here a bomber prototype, the Boeing Y1B-9A, flies with a prototype of the Army's first all-metal monoplane fighter, the Boeing P-26—a much less advanced design.

Right Looking for a fighter design breakthrough, the U.S. Army reviewed a series of unorthodox designs in 1940. Curtiss-Wright proposed a canard-wing pusher, Model 24, and the wood-and-fabric mockup CW-24B flew in December 1941. Full-scale metal versions were tested later, but problems with the inherently unstable canard wing were never resolved.

Facing The family resemblance between Grumman's last Navy biplane, the F3F, and its famous World War II fighter, the F6F, is clear in this postwar photograph. In combat, sturdy Grumman F4Fs and F6Fs were renowned for their ability to withstand damage.

Right The Boeing P-26 Peashooter was the U.S. Army's first all-metal monoplane fighter. It straddled two generations, for it was also the last American fighter with an open cockpit, fixed landing gear, and externally braced wings. In its years of service, fighter designs moved rapidly toward far more deadly configurations. The Peashooter weighed 3,000 pounds and carried two .30 calibre machine guns; its successor in the Army Air Service, the Curtiss P-40 Tomahawk, weighed 8,000 pounds and carried six wing-mounted .50 calibre machine guns.

Facing and Overleaf Sydney Camm of the Hawker Aircraft Company topped his beautiful Fury of 1931 with one of the most important fighters in history, the Hawker Hurricane. Tested in 1935, the Hurricane began to reach RAF squadrons in 1937 and was their principal frontline fighter at the outbreak of war.

Luftwaffe's "Condor Legion" to serve General Franco in the Spanish Civil War, American civilians remained uninterested and our fighter pilots quietly wondered how they would stack up.

One serene afternoon in the summer of 1938, shortly before Hitler bluffed Chamberlain at Munich, a college classmate and I, touring southwestern England, pedaled our laden bicycles past a long hedgerow. A sudden sound intruded—a distant roar, rising in a frighteningly rapid crescendo. Then, with a crash of power that spilled us off our bikes, three planes flashed over our heads, wheels still retracting. We stared at them slack-jawed as they swept past in a V and soared skyward.

These were no racy little orange-winged Peashooters with white-scarved pilots. They were bigger and meaner and much faster—shark-nosed, with thundering, blue-flaming exhaust stacks and olive-drab wings marked only with the bright British rondels. They were new RAF Hurricanes, off on a routine patrol. To us Yanks, they were a revelation. To everyone who glanced at them that peaceful day, they were a somewhat chilling glimpse of the future.

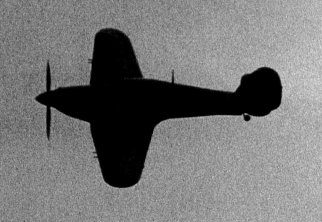

THEIR FINEST HOUR

The early Hurricanes I saw in England could go over 300 miles per hour and climb up to 30,000 feet. They were among the first of the new breed of fighters—planes that Allied governments were lucky to have. Unwilling to invest in a war they hoped would never arrive, politicians put the burden of research and development on aircraft firms. If a plane proved itself in racing competitions and military tests, air forces might buy in.

Striving for these uncertain rewards, companies like Curtiss and Bell in the United States and Supermarine and Hawker in Great Britain began to push past the design limits of the biplanes old-fashioned generals trusted. The story of the Supermarine company was typical. Their sleek little monoplanes, designed by Reginald J. Mitchell, had won the 1927 and 1929 Schneider trophies. For the 1931 race, in which Great Britain had a chance to retire the trophy, a private citizen, Lady Houston, donated £100,000 to improve Supermarine's entry.

Mitchell's Supermarine S-6b, powered by a Rolls-Royce RV-12 engine, blew around the course at an average speed of 340 miles per hour and set a new speed record of 407 miles per hour. Basing his subsequent work on this plane, Mitchell developed the Spitfire, testing a prototype in 1936. The RAF was interested; the plane, with its innovative elliptical wing and Rolls-Royce Merlin engine, climbed and flew even faster than the Hurricane, which the RAF had just begun to purchase.

The Spitfire was a classic, destined to serve through the war with modifications to engines and armament that increased its speed and firepower. Its abilities epitomized what all the most advanced fighter designs of the midthirties—the Hurricane, the Messerschmitt Bf 109, the P-40, the Mitsubishi A6M—reached toward: a monoplane which sacrificed some of the biplane's maneuverability in close combat to achieve vastly improved speed, range, and climbing rates.

In the RAF, the Hurricane was the first to nudge out the still-operational Gloster

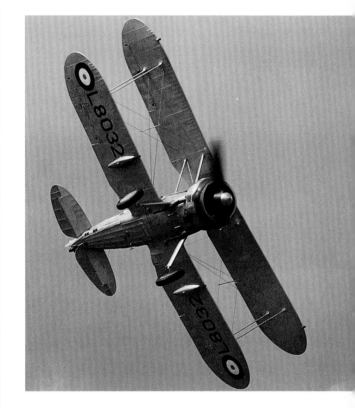

Above At the outbreak of war, Britain struggled to catch up with the German war machine. While squadrons in Britain had new Hurricanes and Spitfires, those elsewhere in the Empire and friendly countries made do with outdated fighters like the Gloster Gladiator of 1934. The results were sometimes surprising. Three Gladiators kept a superior Italian force at bay for days over Malta, and in North Africa and Greece, Marmaduke St. John "Pat" Pattle brought down 23 enemy planes in his Gladiator.

Facing Against the faster Messerschmitt Bf 109, the Hawker Hurricane had two advantages: it could turn more sharply and sustain more damage. Pushing their planes to the limits of their capabilities, RAF pilots in the Battle of Britain managed to blunt the Luftwaffe assault before their own losses grew too high.

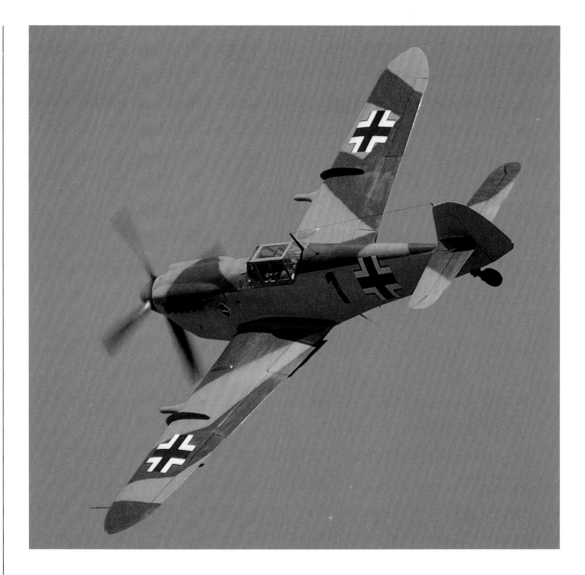

When the first production Messerschmitt Bf 109s appeared in 1937, they had no equal in the world. Their debut in the Spanish Civil War lent urgency to Britain's development of the plane that would be their first rival, the Supermarine Spitfire. Ironically, the Bf 109 prototype of 1935 was driven by a Rolls-Royce Kestrel engine, the power plant of Britain's Hawker Fury. A succession of ever-more powerful Daimler Benz engines propelled the wartime Bf 109s.

Gladiator, a sturdy old workhorse with a strong family resemblance to the Sopwiths and Bristols of 1918. France had a few effective fighters—far fewer than was generally supposed. One, the Morane-Saulnier 406 of 1938, was equal in abilities to the Hurricane. Another was imported from the United States: the Curtiss P-36, a decent performer with a radial Twin Wasp engine. In the U.S. Navy, the newest fighter was still a biplane: the Grumman F3F. And a clunky monoplane, the Brewster Buffalo, was soon to reach some squadrons. But both Army and Navy airmen were eyeing the drawing boards where new designs were taking shape, the F4F Hellcats, P-39 Airacobras, P-40 Warhawks, and P-38 Lightnings that would serve in the first part of the war.

Meanwhile, Germany and Japan were testing their monoplane fighters in combat. Fighting for Franco in the Spanish Civil War, Germany phased out its last biplane fighter, the Heinkel He 51, in favor of the Messerschmitt Bf 109, which, along

Above In 1935, Hitler unveiled the air force he had secretly built up since coming to power. The Heinkel He 51, the Nazi Luftwaffe's first frontline fighter, was supplied to Francisco Franco's Nationalists in Spain in 1936. Then, seizing the chance to test their men and planes in combat, the Nazis sent their own Condor Legion to Spain, equipped at first with more He 51s.

Left The Soviet Union backed the Republicans in Spain, supplying them with the Polikarpov I-15, a sturdy and reliable biplane which outperformed the He 51. Soon, however, the first Messerschmitt Bf 109s reached the Condor Legion, and the I-15 had little chance against the superb monoplane fighter.

Above France scrambled in 1939 to fill the gaps in its long-neglected *Armée de l'Air*. When Hitler invaded in 1940, the Dewoitine D-520, a 1936 design, maintained a 2:1 victory ratio over less maneuverable German opponents. But there weren't enough D-520s to make a difference; when France surrendered on June 22, only 220 had reached the squadrons.

Right So successful was the Messerschmitt Bf 109 at first that work on new and better fighters was not a high priority. Later, the Nazis tried to compensate with sheer numbers. By 1945, 35,000 Bf 109s had been built–more than any other fighter in history.

Facing Italian fighter pilots entered World War II flying the Macchi MC-200 (below), a competent radial-engine fighter which was produced in large numbers. Its designer, Mario Castoldi, would also supply Italy with two of the most promising fighter designs of the war, the Macchi C.202 and the Macchi C.205 (above). The C.205 flew over 400 miles per hour and maneuvered exquisitely. Only 300 were built; by the time of its appearance in 1943, Italian manufacturing was badly handicapped by Allied raids.

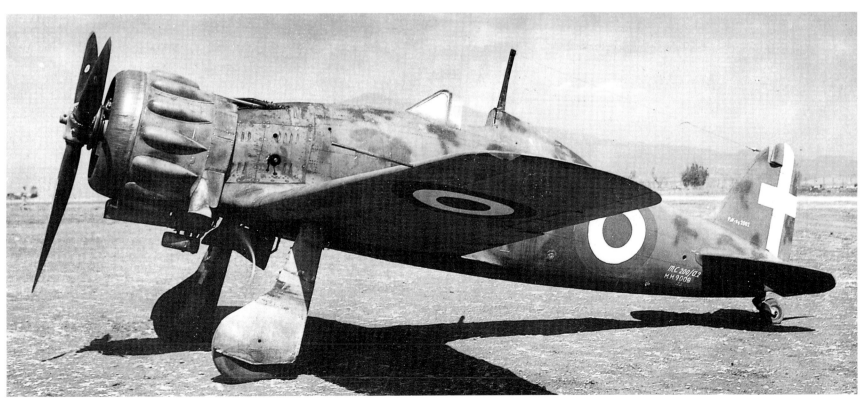

Right Supermarine Spitfires owed some of their speed and handling to their unique elliptical wings. After the war, when aircraft designers sought to break the sound barrier, the shape and thinness of the Spitfire wing were clues to the solution.

Facing Few basic designs in the history of aviation have proved as adaptable as the Spitfire, Reginald Mitchell's last fighter for the Supermarine company. As engines grew more powerful and combat speeds increased in World War II, the Spitfire was continually modified. The Mk. XVI at war's end was twice as heavy and twice as powerful as the Mk. I of 1939. It could reach 20,000 feet in half the earlier plane's time and fired three times as much ammunition per second.

with the Stuka dive bomber, made the Luftwaffe's Condor Legion appear invincible to the rest of the world.

Nobody paid much attention to Japanese aviation in China, where the last of its open-cockpit fighters, the agile Mitsubishi A5M monoplane, was supplemented by a few experimental A6Ms—the first Zeroes. These fighters made short work of China's Russian-supplied Polikarpov I-15s and I-16s.

The second Great War began with a Nazi blitzkrieg in Poland, then slumped into semiconsciousness until the spring of 1940. Erupting again, it roared through Norway and Denmark, the Low Countries, finally France. Messerschmitt Bf 109 pilots, morale soaring, prepared to take on what they considered to be the beaten Royal Air Force.

But by the time bomb-laden Heinkels and Dorniers of the Luftwaffe rumbled across the Channel to start the Battle of Britain, the RAF was anything but beaten. Auxiliary pilots, trained before the war, beefed up the squadrons. Men who had flown for France, Poland, Norway, and other defeated nations switched into RAF blue and set out to avenge their countries. About 700 Hawker Hurricanes were combat-ready. And the new and beautiful Spitfires were now rolling off the assembly lines at a good clip; over 300 had reached the squadrons.

Designed principally to defend England from attack, the Spitfire had one shortcoming—a limited fuel range. With external fuel tanks, later Spitfires could be used to escort bomber sorties over Europe. By then, true long-range fighters like the North American P-51 Mustang and the Republic P-47 Thunderbolt had also come into service.

British fighter pilots had a great advantage in meeting the enemy over their own green fields. Their chief disadvantage was lack of experience. They discovered things as they survived their days: how to scramble, racing out to their ships and jamming them into the air without even checking the magnetos, then climbing fast to meet the enemy bombers. They discovered effective formations, spread out so they could maneuver without colliding. They discovered how to hit at high speed, out of the sun, and break away. They mastered their fast, powerful aircraft and did their best to get the bristling wing guns on target.

Britain's top ace, Johnnie Johnson, wrote *Full Circle*, an overall survey of fighter flying. He mentions that in World War II, deflection shooting was seldom accurate.

Instead of taking the proper lead and triggering off a lethal burst, pilots just tried to get into the enemy's hip pocket and blast him. Even then, the new boys were apt to be skidding or sideslipping so much that their guns just sprayed the general area.

High speed barred the old-fashioned, close-range dogfighting. Yet many precepts from the earlier war remained sound: the value of height, of attacking out of the sun, of turning into the enemy for a head-on pass. German fighters were always above the bombers, prepared to "bounce" the British interceptors as they clawed their way up.

Britain was no place to hold school. At first, German pilots like Werner Mölders who had fought in Spain had a distinct advantage over the untested British. Following Boelcke's tradition, Mölders tried to teach his young colleagues. His friend Adolf Galland tried to sharpen the performance of the whole Luftwaffe.

Galland, a product of secret German training that had sidestepped the Versailles Treaty, learned to fly gliders, then was schooled as a civilian in powered flight. Ironically, many future German war pilots learned military flying in the Soviet Union. Galland was taught in Italy.

Above The cockpit of the Spitfire was spare, rugged, and cramped. The simple instrumentation gave read-outs on engine fluid levels and pressures as well as air speed, altitude, and rate of climb. A convenient switch on the control column fired the guns.

Left James E. "Johnnie" Johnson scored his first victory in a Spitfire over France in 1941 and ended the war as the RAF's top ace with 38 downed enemy aircraft. Remarkably, he scored all of his victories over fighter planes, more agile and challenging quarry than bombers.

Above Douglas Bader reportedly advised his men to "read the diaries of World War I pilots; the fighting techniques they developed were still valid, and a man would live longer if he studied them."

Right During the Battle of Britain, Adolf Galland (left) and other leading Luftwaffe fighter pilots quickly saw the need to change their tactics in response to the unexpectedly ferocious British defense. But their efforts were hampered by the misguided theories of Hitler and his air minister, Hermann Göring (center), who favored bombing missions over direct assaults on RAF fighter squadrons.

A fine acrobatic pilot, he finally cracked up during an inverted buzz job and buried a lot of instruments in his face, badly damaging one eye. The injury should have grounded him. But he memorized the eye chart and in 1938 was posted to the Condor Legion.

Galland hit his stride during the Battle of Britain. A veteran fighter pilot, blooded and scarred, he had no use for the tight formations that looked great in the newsreels. Instead, he wanted his fighters to work in pairs, spread apart so they could support each other. His ideas put him in opposition to his boss, *Reichsmarschall* Hermann Göring, now even more of a self-adoring martinet than he'd been back when he took over Richthofen's squadron. Worried by the losses to his bomber fleet, Göring used to chew out his fighter pilots, then suddenly soften and ask what they needed. Galland got into lots of trouble by answering that he wanted to equip his boys with Spitfires.

Among the British who flew those Spitfires and Hurricanes was the irrepressible Douglas Bader, an inspiration to a generation of Allied pilots. He'd been in the RAF back when it was "the world's best flying club." He played cricket on spotless ovals, dressed for dinner, and flew impeccable acrobatics in Gloster biplanes until he hit the ground and ended up with two artificial legs. That put him out of flying until the new war erupted.

Back in the cockpit for the Battle of Britain, this old pro inspired younger pilots

with his cool-headed competence—legs or no—and distressed Fighter Command with his equally cool disobedience of what he considered inane orders. Eventually shot down and taken prisoner, Bader was royally greeted by Galland. The two enemies chatted amiably and the German promised to try to get Bader's best legs dropped by parachute (to fly, he made do with second best). Galland also showed Bader his Messerschmitt Bf 109 and let him sit in the cockpit.

"Let me do just one circle over the airfield," begged the Englishman. Galland reported that he nearly gave in.

The Battle of Britain was by no means the one-sided British victory that news reports called it at the time. The RAF lost heavily, but damaged the Luftwaffe enough that Hitler called off his invasion of Britain. The battle was won by fighter pilots.

The fighter pilots of World War II were not the wild adventurers who had risked their necks by simply climbing into the aircraft of 1914. This was a new breed, professional, competent, who all did their job in about the same way, shared common problems, and experienced the same rewards and frustrations whether they flew a

Like the Spitfire, the Messerschmitt Bf 109 took well to continued improvement in power and armament. In combat over Britain, the two planes were evenly matched. If Spitfires could maneuver better (a claim which Luftwaffe pilots sometimes disputed), the Messerschmitts' Daimler-Benz engines were distinctly more powerful at high altitudes.

The Curtiss P-40 Warhawk was slower and less agile than the Messerschmitt Bf 109, the Supermarine Spitfire, or the Mitsubishi A6M Zero. Its sturdiness compensated for some of its faults, and while more up-to-date American designs were still being tested, the Curtiss company was ready in 1941 to mass-produce their proven fighter. Soon thousands of Warhawks ("Tomahawks" in the RAF) were going out to British and American squadrons in North Africa and the Far East and to Soviet squadrons on the Eastern Front.

Above The Messerschmitt Bf 109 was dangerous for novices, especially during landings and takeoffs. The landing gear, set closely together, was little help in balancing the Bf 109's strong prop torque, and the slightest error on takeoffs or landings could cause the plane to twist off course and crash.

Left In May 1940, the RAF asked North American, a small California aircraft firm, to manufacture Curtiss P-40s under license. The firm made a counteroffer: a faster, more heavily armed fighter with the same engine, the Allison V-1710. Within four months, North American completed a prototype of the P-51 Mustang, which would become one of the war's finest fighters. In early variants, the roof of the cockpit was flush with the aft fuselage.

Above Luftwaffe ace Erich Hartmann began his career slowly, not scoring a victory until his 91st sortie over the Russian front. By the end of the war, he had shot down 352 Soviet planes—more aircraft than any other fighter pilot in history.

Right Hans Marseille, one of Germany's greatest aces, was especially known for his brilliant marksmanship and flying skills. He is said to have worn tennis shoes in the cockpit to improve his feel for the rudder pedals. Fighting principally in North Africa, he compiled a total of 158 victories. And in nine hours on September 1, 1942, he knocked down 17 British P-40s, Hurricanes, and Spitfires.

Hurricane or a Messerschmitt Bf 109, a Macchi or a Zeke. They were all cut from the same cloth, no matter the color of the uniform. Put them all together in a situation where they weren't trying to kill each other, and, in the common language of their guild, they would have talked up a storm.

Just as World War I fighter pilots evolved from lone hunters to disciplined squadron members, World War II flyers were coordinated into ever-larger strategic units. In *Full Circle*, Johnnie Johnson traces the change from the early days, when air fighting over Britain and France was a high-speed, heavy-gunned continuation of World War I dogfighting, to the warfare of 1944 and 1945, when air armies of 2,000 bombers escorted by nearly 1,000 fighters fought their Battles of Verdun and the Somme four miles high in the smoky sky.

No World War II pilot of any country won the public adulation of a Guynemer or a Ball. "Red Baron" has become part of our language. But few people have ever heard of Erich Hartmann, who fought for Germany in the later war and claimed more than four times as many victories as Richthofen.

Brilliant as he was, Hartmann owed his incredible score in part to his assignment on the Eastern Front. There he had the chance to learn—a luxury denied

many Battle of Britain warriors, who fell rapidly against equally skilled opponents. Fighting inexperienced Soviet flyers, Hartmann knocked down 352 enemy aircraft.

In the West, Soviet aces are almost unremembered. They deserve more recognition; they had to learn faster than anyone and recover from the most staggering early losses of any Ally. During the first week of the Nazi invasion in June 1941, the Luftwaffe demolished some 4,000 Soviet combat aircraft. Most of them were shot up on the ground.

The flyers that got in the air, mostly in Polikarpov I-16s, open-cockpit mono-planes from 1937, were outclassed by the Luftwaffe in their Messerschmitt Bf 109s. Desperate to make a dent in the Nazi onslaught, one Lieutenant Ivanov rammed a Bf 110 with his I-16 on the first day of the offensive. Eight other Soviet fighters also rammed Luftwaffe aircraft that day.

Returning to base after shooting down his 300th enemy aircraft, Erich Hartmann received a lively welcome from his squadron. The prodigious victory tallies of German aces on the Russian front were due in part to the Soviets' hastily trained pilots. At the same time, the Luftwaffe rarely rotated veteran fighters from combat to flight instruction. German pilots flew until they were killed, captured, or critically wounded; Hartmann had chalked up 1,500 missions when Germany surrendered, and Hans Ulrich-Rudel, a Stuka flyer, survived 2,530—an all-time record.

ДА ЗДРАВСТВУЕТ ВЕЛИКИЙ ПОЛКОВОДЕЦ ОТЕЧЕСТВЕННОЙ ВОЙНЫ т. СТАЛИН

Above The Soviet aircraft industry worked feverishly to replace the disastrous losses of 1941. To conserve metal and save weight, Aleksandr Yakovlev's Yak-7b, a fighter of 1942, was partly sheathed in plywood.

Left At first, Soviet fighter pilots were thoroughly demoralized by the Luftwaffe's impressive aircraft and relentless tactics—and by their own unreliable planes. Training programs in 1942 and 1943 taught them to keep formation and to maneuver more aggressively. With the new Yaks of 1943, they began providing effective air cover for the Red Army.

Facing Through Lend-Lease, the United States supplied about 4,700 Bell P-39 Airacobras to the Soviet Union—almost half of all the P-39s produced. The plane had several unique features: a 37mm cannon was fitted inside the hollow propeller shaft, poking out through the nose, and the engine, the ubiquitous Allison V-1710, was mounted behind the pilot in the center of the fuselage.

Above Ivan Kozhedub, the top-scoring Soviet fighter pilot (and Allied ace), shot down 62 German planes—including a Messerschmitt Me 262 jet fighter. Recklessness almost killed Kozhedub in his first aerial combat at Kursk on July 6, 1943, but he learned quickly: two Messerschmitts and two Stukas fell to his guns in the next three days.

Right Artem Mikoyan and Mikhail Gurevich, designers of some of the Soviet Union's most important fighters in the last 40 years, began their collaboration at the start of World War II. The MiG-3, their second fighter, appeared at the end of 1941. At high altitudes, its performance equaled the best fighters of the day. Closer to earth, the Yak-1 pleased Soviet airmen more.

The trick was to survive the collision and bail out. Those who succeeded were often made Heroes of the Soviet Union; one, Boris Kobzan, survived four rammings during the war. Needless to say, the Soviet air command encouraged the technique only with obsolete planes.

In German eyes, Soviet pilots were never a match. But by 1943, Soviet pilots, whose training had improved dramatically, began to be supplied with fighters that could make a difference. Gradually, they began turning back the Luftwaffe. The early closed-cockpit monoplanes, the MiG-3 and the LaGG-3, both plagued with difficulties, gave way to the fast, maneuverable Yak-1, the prototype for the Soviets' best wartime fighters.

Help also came from abroad; Great Britain sent Hurricanes; the United States sent P-40s and P-39s. Soviet aces especially liked the P-39; Aleksandr Pokryshkin, the second-ranking Red ace with 59 victories, often scored in the Airacobra, which Soviets called *Britchik*, "Little Shaver."

Unlike Soviet air battles, the Battle of Britain was well reported in the United States, and the stories affected those Americans who thought they might soon be involved. If war came, I—and millions like me—wanted to fly. So we eagerly read of "Cobber" Kain, the New Zealander, of "Paddy" Finucane's marksmanship, of "Sailor" Malan, the South African who, like Boelcke, laid out rules for air fighting. We read Richard Hillary's *Falling Through Space* and John MacGee's moving poem, "High Flight." We even imitated the understatement of these new heroes: "Actually, I had

Above Aleksandr Yakovlev's series of fighters, the Yak-1, Yak-3, Yak-7, and Yak-9, gave Soviet pilots a chance to meet the Luftwaffe on equal terms. The Yak-3 (shown in flight) reached combat in 1943. Designed as an interceptor, it performed so well at lower altitudes that it was reassigned to ground-attack squadrons. Below 10,000 feet, it flew better than the Messerschmitt Bf 109 and the Focke-Wulf Fw 190.

Left Yakovlev's best-known wartime design was the Yak-9, which military historians rank with the Spitfire and the Bf 109 as one of the war's most significant fighters. Seventeen thousand were built; the Yak-9DD variant shown was equipped to fly long-range missions with external fuel tanks.

Above and Facing The safe, reliable North American AT-6 was the Allies' most widely used advanced trainer in World War II. Known as the Texan in the United States and the Harvard in Great Britain, the AT-6 had the feel and weight of a small fighter, and its narrow landing gear challenged pilots' landing abilities. The versatile aircraft also served in combat; an early version, Australia's Commonwealth Wirraway, flew light bombing and reconnaissance missions in World War II, and late-model AT-6s flew reconnaissance in Korea, targeting strike sites for fighter-bombers. Even as recently as the 1970s, T-6s in the air forces of a number of smaller nations flew missions against rebel forces.

Above The North American P-51D Mustang carried six .50-calibre wing-mounted machine guns, two more than earlier versions. The P-51D was also the first variant with a bubble canopy, which widened the pilot's field of vision.

Facing Massive strategic bombing was the primary goal of the Allied air forces in Europe. Early in the war, fighters lacked the range of bombers, and bombers flew missions into Germany unescorted—an extremely hazardous undertaking. With the advent of long-range fighters like the P-51, the Allies began to strike vital German targets with deadly regularity in 1944. Here, at a recent air show reenactment, four P-51s cover a B-17 Flying Fortress.

Above American ace Robert Johnson flew a Republic P-47 Thunderbolt with Colonel Hubert Zemke's "Wolfpack," the 56th Fighter Group. Johnson ended the war as the United States' fourth-ranking ace with 28 victories. Along with their rivals, Colonel Don Blakeslee's 4th Fighter Group, the 56th escorted some of the first large-scale American bomber flights over Berlin in 1944.

Facing An aerodynamic innovation called the low-drag airfoil contributed greatly to the performance of the North American P-51 Mustang. Most wings of the time were thickest near the leading edge, creating high drag over most of the wing surface in flight. The low-drag airfoil was thickest near the middle; the leading edge cut smoothly into the air, and drag was less pronounced.

Above If the P-51 was a thoroughbred, the Republic P-47 Thunderbolt was a quarter horse—tough, reliable, predictable. Its nicknames—Jug, Seven-ton Milk Bottle—suggest its lack of glamor. But pilots who benefited from its ability to withstand combat damage became converts. Equipped with the powerful Pratt & Whitney Double Wasp radial engine, the Thunderbolt excelled in rapid climbs and powered dives, and was remarkably agile for its size and weight. Allied pilots in Thunderbolts spearheaded the crippling of the Luftwaffe in 1943 and 1944—blowing the roof off of Hitler's "Fortress Europe."

Right Allied flyers began meeting a formidable new fighter over Europe in 1941, the Focke-Wulf Fw 190. Nicknamed *Wuerger*, the Butcherbird, the Fw 190 was a much easier plane to fly than the Messerschmitt Bf 109. Its design was flexible enough to accommodate the switch from a BMW radial engine to a more powerful Junkers Jumo inline late in 1943.

rather a good afternoon—seven Jerries in five minutes. Am I late for tea?"

In 1942, young Americans began pouring into the European skies, all healthy and boisterous, all splendidly trained. They flew good planes, produced by the thousands. The bomber crews proved themselves the truest heroes: no fighter pilot can quite picture the guts it took to surge steadily ahead, straight and level, through those curtains of flak.

Many eager Americans trained in Canada before Pearl Harbor. Some went into action as members of the RAF's Eagle squadrons. Don Blakeslee joined the Eagles in 1941 and rose to command a squadron. When the Yanks arrived, he transferred to the Eighth Air Force. At first he hated trading in his lively, lovely Spitfire for a seven-ton P-47, but after tangling successfully with Germany's deadly FW-190 squadrons from Abbeville and St. Omer, he felt better. His husky "Jug" brought him back to Britain, though its engine was ripped by cannon fire.

Blakeslee commanded the Fourth Fighter Group, organized from Eagle Squadron members. The story goes that before his transfer he was demoted from squadron leader to flying officer. The American brass wondered why, and were told that a sudden inspection had flushed two sprightly WAAFs out of his bedroom window. "Two!" exclaimed General Monk Hunter, Eighth Air Force fighter commander. "Hell, make him a colonel!"

One of Blakeslee's pilots, high-scoring Don Gentile, developed an uncanny

Above Francis K. "Gabby" Gabreski was one of the aces flying Republic P-47 Thunderbolts in Hubert Zemke's Wolfpack. Gabreski's World War II flying experience went all the way back to Pearl Harbor, where his P-40 squadron had struggled to pursue the Japanese from Wheeler Field. Transferred to England in 1942, he became the leading American ace in Europe, with 31 downed German aircraft to his credit. Flying a ground-attack mission late in July 1944, he grazed a field with his propeller, crash-landed, and was taken prisoner.

Left In the tradition of the Lafayette Escadrille, a number of Americans volunteered with the RAF at the start of World War II. The first Eagle Squadron, the 71st, took shape after the Battle of Britain. Its combat record for the first nine months was uninspiring—one Hurricane shot down by accident. A new commander in mid-1941 sharpened performance. In RAF fighter sweeps over Normandy and Brittany, the Eagle squadrons had destroyed more than 70 enemy aircraft when the USAAF absorbed them in 1942, creating the elite 4th Fighter Group around a nucleus of these veterans.

Above Don Gentile flew P-51s with Blakeslee's 4th Fighter Group, and destroyed 30 Nazi planes before being shipped home to boost morale and train new pilots in May 1944. After one raid on Berlin, Gentile allegedly quipped, "There were so many planes up there today that we were choosy about which ones we shot down."

Right The first black pilots in American military aviation, the 99th Fighter Squadron, trained at Tuskegee Air Base in Alabama in 1940 and 1941. Stationed first in Tunisia, then in Sicily and Italy, the 99th flew P-40s, P-39s, and P-47s before receiving P-51s in 1944. In Italy, the 99th and three other black squadrons formed the 332nd Fighter Group. Escorting bombing missions over Germany, the 332nd was credited with never losing a bomber to enemy fighters.

Facing In the P-51D, the most numerous version of the Mustang, a Rolls-Royce Merlin engine replaced the Allison V-1710, and the plane's speed and performance improved dramatically.

rapport with his friend John Godfrey. Flying as an element, they worked together so well that Göring vowed he would sacrifice two crack squadrons to get them.

Americans had crack squadrons too. One day after I had returned from overseas, I boarded a wartime train and sat next to a member of one of them. He was a trim young black with Army wings on his tunic. "Ninety-ninth?" I asked, and he nodded.

Everyone knew about this first all-black squadron whose members had braved the usual racism of those days to win their chance to fight in the air. "How did you make out?" I asked. "Not too hot," he said. "I only got eight." That was seven better than I'd done, but I realized that this bunch had special standards. They were intent on turning a grudging experiment into a resounding success. Their teamwork and bravery exemplified the fighter pilot's contribution to the war.

THE WAR IN THE PACIFIC

All Pacific carrier squadrons were crack, for my money. Picture the tension in the ready room before a mission. Over the intercom, a voice barks: "Pilots, man your planes!" and the flyers dash to the flight deck, where flight crews help plane after plane take to the air.

Navy fighter pilots navigated accurately over the featureless sea, identified their enemy, and fought them with precision and discipline. Then they had to find their way back to the carrier, often shot up and short of fuel, and get their planes down on a heaving flight deck, sometimes after dark and in blackout conditions. Anyone who could do all that was an ace, no matter what his score.

Early in the war, the Japanese Zero dominated Pacific skies from the Marianas to the Solomons and from Sumatra to the tail of New Guinea, shocking American, Australian, Dutch, and British airmen with their devilish performance: a quick, steep climb; a turn that was simply a pirouette; the smashing impact of well-aimed cannonfire. Flying thus, Hiroyoshi Nishizawa and Saburo Sakai racked up scores of 87 and 61 respectively.

The Japanese taught American flyers some new tricks in the Pacific theaters. Their nimble planes were built to dogfight, and their pilots tried to sucker us into playing that game. In head-on passes, the Japanese were almost suicidally fearless. Usually, however, they were wheeling and weaving above us, and if we climbed toward them, they'd often half roll all at once and come blazing down. P-38s handled them with a straight pass, a shallow dive too fast for them to follow, then a shallow climb.

Over the Coral Sea in May 1942, superbly trained American naval pilots proved the Zero beatable. So did Claire Chennault's American Volunteer Group, the Flying Tigers. Chennault had been in China since 1936, training the Chinese air force. In 1941, alarmed by the increasing Japanese threat to Burma and India, he traveled to the United States and recruited skilled fighter pilots from all the services. Flying P-40s, the AVG was ready to fight in November, but didn't get into action until two weeks after Pearl Harbor.

Above Known as "the Devil" to his fellow pilots, Hiroyoshi Nishizawa was Japan's top ace. His career ended unluckily; after he ferried a spare fighter to a neighboring squadron, the transport he hitched a ride home in was shot down with no survivors.

Facing Ten thousand Zeroes were built in World War II, but only two, including the one shown here, exist today. Remarkably, the Zero achieved its performance with an engine less powerful than any of its adversaries—780 horsepower in the prototype A6M1, 1,130 in the final A6M7. To get the most out of the engine, designer Jiro Horikoshi created an unusually light airframe. That lightness would handicap the Zero later; it was much more susceptible to combat damage than the Hellcats, Wildcats, and Lightnings it faced in the Pacific.

Right The Grumman F4F Wildcat was the Navy's frontline fighter at the time of Pearl Harbor, and it remained so until 1943, when the first Grumman F6F Hellcats appeared. The plane exemplified Roy Grumman's design philosophy: "Make it strong, make it work, and make it simple." Capitalizing on the Wildcat's ruggedness, Navy pilots developed formation tactics and diving passes which helped them hold their own against the Zero.

Right A Navy photographer looks back over the rudder of a plane as others follow it from the deck of USS *Saratoga* in February 1943. In the Pacific theater, the United States and Japan virtually invented the art of carrier warfare. At the Battle of the Coral Sea in May 1942, ships fought without coming in range and firing upon each other—a first in naval history. Instead, dive-bombers struck at enemy ships while fighters dueled above them. Five other carrier engagements— the world's only battles between carriers—followed until Japan's naval forces were finally crushed at the Battle of Leyte Gulf in October 1944.

Facing, above Grumman designed the F6F Hellcat specifically to drive the Zero from the skies of the Pacific. Based on the sturdy Wildcat, the Hellcat could climb faster, fly faster, fly farther, and take more punishment than its predecessor. Pilots in Hellcats destroyed 5,155 Japanese planes while losing only 280 of their own—a 19:1 kill ratio unmatched by any other combat plane.

Facing, below One tactic American pilots in Wildcats and Hellcats used against the Zero was called the "Thach Weave," after Lieutenant Commander John S. "Jimmy" Thach. If Zeroes were pursuing both members of an element, the Americans turned toward each other and fired as the other's Zero zoomed into their sights. The Thach Weave enabled pilots in the slower Grummans to use deflection shooting against the Zero, which they could not have overtaken or evaded in a straight chase.

Above The F6F Hellcat's mechanical reliability endeared it to carrier airmen. On average, over 90 percent of all frontline Hellcats were ready and available for combat duty—an unmatched record. Taken on board the USS *Saratoga*, this photograph of 1943 or 1944 shows crewmen chocking the wheels of newly returned Hellcats as others approach the flight deck after a mission.

Left Several multiple victories helped Commander David McCampbell become the Navy's top ace in World War II. On June 19, 1944, he shot down seven planes. And during the Battle of Leyte Gulf, the last stand for Japan's carrier forces, his tally for October 24 alone was nine.

Facing In combat, there are no routine landings on a carrier. Here, on board the USS *Essex*, the arresting wires have stopped a battle-damaged Grumman F6F Hellcat.

Chennault's AVG was a volatile mix of tough individualists. Among them was a burly ex-Marine, Gregory Boyington, who downed six planes in his P-40, raised hell in the air and on the ground, managed to make Chennault despise him, but finally returned to the Corps and raised his score to 28 in the renowned "Black Sheep" squadron before getting shot down and taken prisoner. "Pappy" Boyington was a driven man and drove his squadron hard and well. Any similarity between the real Black Sheep and the television program about them is purely coincidental.

Ex-Flying Tigers had priceless information for new Army and Navy pilots who were about to tangle with the Japanese, and they usually shared it generously. I still remember the briefing sessions with a red-headed former Tiger on a troopship in the Pacific when I was one of 300 early replacements, headed, it turned out, for New Guinea.

"When you see them wheeling around, generally above you, slam your throttle through the gate and climb all you can," he'd say. "When they come down, try to dive through them, balls out. Take a shot where you can and keep going in a shallow dive. When you're out of range, pull up and come back at them the same way. Hit and run. If you turn, they'll get you. Remember, a Zeke or an Oscar can make two turns inside your one."

In the strange war over New Guinea, the problem was often Step One: seeing the Zeroes. I knew pilots who never saw one in months of operations. Perhaps the Japanese could have mounted a modest air army in New Guinea late in 1942, when

Above The AVG's P-40s were technically inferior to Japan's Nakajima Ki-43 Hayabusas ("Oscars") over China. Nonetheless, making the most of the Warhawk's rugged construction and dependability, the Flying Tigers shot down 286 enemy aircraft in the first six months of 1942 while losing only 23 of their own.

Left With its long nose, bent wings, and big propeller, the Chance Vought F4U Corsair was one of the war's most noticeable planes. The Navy signed contracts for the F6F Hellcat and the F4U on the same day in 1941, but the more complex Corsair took a year longer to reach the squadrons.

Above Grumman's hefty F7F Tigercat was the finest twin-engine fighter of the war, but reached Okinawa too late to be used in combat. In the Korean War, it would serve as a long-range night fighter and strike aircraft.

Left Lockheed's twin-boom design for the famous P-38 inspired the North American F-82 Twin Mustang. Planned as a fast, long-range escort for the B-29 Superfortress, the F-82 missed World War II, but flew ground attack and night missions in Korea.

Facing With two 2,000 horsepower radial engines, the Northrop P-61 Black Widow night fighter had the power to fly at 350 miles per hour hauling heavy radar equipment. Never practical before radar, night fighting became a serious and deadly game in World War II. Early radar screens were tricky to decipher, and Allied and Nazi pilots strove to outwit each other with jamming and other electronic tricks.

Right No one flew Lockheed's P-38 better than Dick Bong, the United States' top ace in World War II with 40 victories. Laconic and unassuming, Bong compensated for his allegedly poor gunnery with outstanding eyesight and a willingness to fly very near his target. After he became the first American pilot to top Eddie Rickenbacker's score, he was reassigned to advanced combat instruction. Taking new pilots on practice flights in the Southwest Pacific, he bent the rules and bagged another 13 enemy planes.

Facing The twin-boomed, two-engine Lockheed P-38 Lightning was a new answer to a familiar problem in propeller-driven fighter design: how to get better performance without building a more powerful engine. The U.S. Army Air Forces sought a better fighter than the P-39 and P-40, but couldn't count on a more powerful engine than those fighters' Allison V-1710s. By putting two Allisons on one light and sturdy airframe, Lockheed achieved the needed jump in performance—and entered the military aircraft market. In World War II, American pilots would destroy more Japanese aircraft from P-38s than from any other plane.

I joined my P-39 squadron. But for them, as for us, New Guinea's diseases, heat, storms, and mountains were the greatest enemies. Both sides had to beat these before they could meet each other.

Army squadrons found New Guinea a backwater of the war; we were often isolated from each other, and it was hard to believe that somewhere the sky was black with planes. But Dick Bong, the top American ace, found enough here to down 40.

New Guinea was like a small town—sooner or later you met everyone—and I met Bong, a pleasant and modest young midwesterner. He said he was a lousy shot. He said he could only score by yanking his P-38 into exactly the right place. He used to buzz the strip with both engines silent, both propellers feathered, pull into a loop, pop his wheels and flaps when he was on top, and then finish the loop by landing the plane.

Bong admitted that he sought, and received, especially productive missions, and that engineers took special care of his red-nosed '38. In my squadron, our engineering officer struggled to keep 16 planes functioning in jungle encampments where mechanics changed engines with a chain hoist lashed high up on the slanting trunk of a palm tree. With pills to fend off malaria and dysentery, our flight surgeon tried

Another plane built around an engine—and a propeller—was the Chance Vought F4U Corsair. In 1938, Pratt & Whitney introduced the Double Wasp radial engine, with two rows of cylinders. This promising engine required a propeller with a large arc—over 13 feet. To keep the propeller off the ground, the plane's nose needed to be kept unusually high. The normal solution, longer landing gear, would not be sturdy enough for military landings, especially on a carrier. The Vought solution, the inverted gull wing, angled the wing root downward so that short landing gear could be attached at the lowest point.

to keep maybe 24 of the pilots healthy enough for long days of patrols, escorts, and ground attacks, sometimes three missions a day.

Strangely, morale soared and lasting friendships were welded in this world of intense discomfort—and, ironically, great beauty. We shared the certain knowledge of hidden danger. We also sensed drama in our lives....

You wake to the whirr of a watchman's rattle and the voice of the charge of quarters: "First flight! First flight!" Even in your restless sleep, you've expected the call, for last night, your name was posted number four on Red Flight, the early patrol. You'd rather lead the rear element than be last man, but this is the C.O.'s flight, and he wants Wiggins, a flight leader, to take the second element. That puts you on Wiggins' wing— Tail Ass Charlie. The perfect place, you muse as you roll out of your sack, for an everyday GI pilot, the essence of mediocrity, which is all you will ever be.

You pull on a pair of khakis hacked into shorts with your hunting knife. Your sweat-stained flying suit hangs on the tent pole where you hoped it would dry after yesterday's missions. You find it in the dark and shake it to get the bugs out. The sound wakes your tentmate, who will be taking off in Yellow Flight in two hours. "Luck," he murmurs. "Go back to sleep," you say. "I'll see you up there."

You bang the heels of your GI boots and shake them before putting them on. Scorpions like to crawl into boots. Then you clip your hunting knife into the little sleeve you made for it on the inside of your right shin. Your shoulder holster with the big old Colt hangs on the frame of your cot. You strap it on, then smooth out your single, double-folded blanket so the sweat will dry and tuck your mosquito bar under it to keep things out of your bed. You've done this ever since you found a small snake curled up there just as you were getting in.

The mess tent smells of strong coffee—the best part of breakfast. A corporal dumps an eight-inch pancake on a tin plate, adds a thick slab of almost-raw bacon, smears butter on the side, and ladles syrup over the whole thing. The butter is ersatz. It looks like wax. It tastes like wax. The syrup is hot water and sugar solution. You carry the thing to a table and join the C.O. in pecking at it. "After the war, I'm going to eat," he says, "I'm going to eat myself right into an early grave."

You get a little food into your wizened belly and wash down an Atabrine pill with a gulp of lime juice (known as "battery acid"). The flight's other two pilots come in out of the dark. Wiggins sits down beside you and makes an obscene remark about

The Marines were the first to fly the Corsair in combat. Pilots in Gregory Boyington's "Black Sheep" squadron, shown here scrambling for their Corsairs from the alert shack, showed what the "Bent-wing Bird" could do by shooting down 47 Japanese aircraft in their first month of combat.

the food. McLain is a replacement, and the rest of you try to be nice to him because it's hard to be new. Also, if he lasts, he'll allow one of the old guys to be sent home. Like all new pilots, McLain will be the C.O.'s wingman.

A jeep takes the four of you to the flight line, a quarter-mile away, where the jungle's night noises are swallowed by the Allison engines running up. Flashes of blue light from the exhaust stacks stab the darkness.

In the alert tent, dimly lit by a kerosene lantern, the C.O. talks to you for a moment. "Remember, we're the first flight. For an hour, we'll be the only planes over the area, so anything you see will be a bandit. Keep your places. Keep your heads turning." This is for McLain's sake. You and Wiggins don't need to be told.

As you walk to your revetment, the first faint flush of dawn brightens the sky. It will come on fast. There's not much twilight in the tropics. Your crew chief waits by your plane. "Nice day for it, Lieutenant," he says as he boosts you onto the wing. Your Mae

West hangs on the door of the P-39 with your helmet and goggles. Your parachute is in the bucket seat. You don the Mae West, ease inside, and the crew chief helps you snap on chute, safety harness, radio, and oxygen leads. With a pat on your shoulder, he jumps down, leaving you firmly trussed.

Once the helmet's earphones are in place, outside noises fade. The starting of your engine is only a rumble, half lost in the crackling of the radio. You see the other planes rolling out to the end of the strip, and with a wave to the crew chief, you follow. The first element snarls down the runway, propellers leaving spiral streamers of condensation hanging behind. Wiggins pulls into place and you move to his right, your cockpit about even with his tail.

You run a quick magneto check, try your pitch control, then see Wiggins' ailerons flap as a signal to go. Eyes glued on his plane, you start with it, easing your throttle forward to hold position. When his wheels begin tucking up, you realize that you too are airborne, and you feel for your wheel switch and toggle it up. He banks toward you. You both are turning to the right inside the first element, and in a moment, you and Wiggins slide in beside the other two. Climbing on course, your element crosses under to take position on its left, and you cross under Wiggins to fly his left wing. Your flight is now in "finger formation," the planes taking the positions of four spread finger tips. You're maybe 150 yards apart, and it's time to look around.

At first, you marvel at the early morning, the soft light, the distant, jagged mountains, the smoothness of the air, the fresh feel of it in the brightening day, the zest of being in it. Then you focus your eyes on one patch of sky after another. You find a cloud silvered by the sunrise and follow its contours, searching for those little dark dots that could be Zeroes. You turn your head like an owl's until you can see your own rudder, while holding position with peripheral vision.

And so it goes for two grueling hours. Cramped buttocks, a slimy oxygen mask that smells of last night's bully beef, a dazzling sun that you block out with your thumb when you search that quarter, an empty sky. And suddenly your hot, tired eyes catch something. Dots. Four of them. You can't identify them, but they don't *feel* like Zeroes, so you don't call them in.

But McLain does: "Beaver Red, nine o'clock level!"

Instantly a new voice breaks in: "Beaver Red from Beaver Yellow: we have you. We are with you."

The four dots become P-39s, banking toward you. Their nose cannons swing

Facing "Never attempt to dogfight the Zero," concluded American military experts after testing a captured A6M2 in 1942. The American solution was to leave acrobatics to the Zero and build planes with superior speed and power. In the end, like the *Dreidecker* when it met with faster Sopwith Camels, Spads, and S.E. 5as, the Zero no longer gave its pilots the ability to control the terms of the conflict, to choose when to start a fight and when to break it off. The replica shown here is built around the North American AT-6 Harvard trainer.

The U.S. Army Air Force couldn't send its best new planes to all the squadrons at once. In Burma, where the 10th Air Force strove to hold the line against the Japanese, fighter pilot Don Lopez flew P-40 Warhawks until 1944 against better Japanese Nakajima Ki-43 Oscars. Lopez made ace nonetheless, and lived to write a memoir, *Into the Teeth of the Tiger.*

right on you as they turn, giving these beautiful but rather useless little planes a momentarily lethal look. You chuckle, wondering if a Japanese pilot was ever frightened by the sight of a P-39. Probably not.

With a mutual waggle of wings, you part from Yellow Flight and speed back to your base, letting down as you go. Nearing the strip, you tack onto each other in a tight echelon, stepped up from the C.O. so that he can get nice and low without running the rest of you into the ground. He buzzes the strip, kicking up dust with his prop, then flicks upward in a steep climbing turn, streamers creaming off his wingtips. McLain follows, then Wiggins, then you.

The Gs press you into your seat and pull your cheeks down from your eyeballs. Then, cocked on your side in a vertical turn, you snap flap and wheel switches, and the plane whines in protest at the rupture of its sleek lines. You keep it in a close, steep turn until the steel matting of the strip gleams before you, very near. Gently, you bring it straight just in time to raise the nose and feel for the strip.

You are very tired. You unzip your flying suit, tying the arms around your waist. Half naked, you lie on a cot in the alert tent as the sun builds its heat. Someone shouts "kai-kai"—pidgin English for food—and you rise and shamble to a muddy truck with a shiny vat of coffee. It tastes fine. You wash down two brick-hard ship's biscuits smeared with canned peanut butter. This serves as your lunch because in half an hour you are on your second patrol, relieving Blue Flight.

On this one, you see dots again, and this time you call them in instantly. Back in World War I, Canada's great ace, Billy Bishop, wrote that enemy planes soon became easy to identify. "You learn to sense their presence." Right on.

The tiny shapes are like pencil lines in the distant air, fragile, faint, vanishing, then reappearing at three o'clock high. The C.O. comes back: "I got 'em Four. Don't drop your tanks, boys." You watch the spots and climb toward them. They pay no attention. You swivel your head to clear Wiggins' tail, and seeking the bandits again, you find them nearby and overhead, six light bombers with a swarm of Oscars above them.

You see the C.O.'s belly tank tumble away, and you quickly switch and drop yours. The plane feels wonderfully spry without it. All fatigue leaves you. You fly smoothly, confidently. And when your leader pulls up his nose to fire, you do the same, bringing the sight onto a V of bombers, white bottoms against the dark blue sky, huge bright red circles on the wings that seem to shout: "Enemy! Danger!"

Of course they're out of range, but what the hell? You press your trigger anyway, feeling the cannon thump, the propeller-synchronized '50s roar in front of you. The cockpit fills with acrid smoke and you weep inside your goggles, but not before you see the sky above the bombers flash silver as every Oscar snaps over on his back and split-S's down upon you, wings winking with gunfire.

Without a word being said, your flight peels off downward and races for the deck, far faster than any Japanese fighter can dive. And then you must head for the barn; flying on main tanks alone, you'll soon be dry.

The C.O. calls base to send your relief flight. You lean the mixture and coast home, landing with a few gallons left. The rest of the squadron is on the strip to watch you, alerted by the distinctive whistling of the guns, whose protective tape has been blown away. That means you've been shooting at something.

A friend jumps on your wing after you shut down. "Didjagetany?" he asks. All

Pilots sometimes discover capabilities in their planes that official manuals overlook. It was widely held that no American plane could match Japan's Zeroes and Oscars in a turning fight or turn inside the enemy's turn. At low altitudes and speeds near stalling, however, the P-38 revealed that it could match the turning radius of the Zero; its twin counter-rotating engines minimized torque and kept the plane from spinning out.

Above As F4U Corsairs began to reach Pacific squadrons, American success rates rapidly improved. But the Corsair exacted a price for its exhilarating performance. Pilots found they needed twice the usual training time to master it, and noncombat crashes accounted for over half of all Corsairs lost in World War II—giving rise to the nickname "the bent-wing eliminator."

Facing The Republic P-47 Thunderbolt excelled both at high-altitude interception and low-altitude dive-bombing, and was used in all theaters of the war.

one word. You shake your head as you climb out. Oddly, your knees are trembling.

You don't want a third mission, but maintenance is a problem, and good planes are hard to find. So up you go again in the evening—a short mission, because you're not equipped for darkness. Many instruments have been ripped out to save weight.

Finally home, you shower under a pierced belly tank, then take a few long pulls of squadron whiskey. It restores you, even helps you swallow the inevitable bully beef. Before you turn in, there's a briefing about tomorrow. You find yourself posted again. Element leader, this time.

You shake out your blanket, scan the air mattress with a flashlight, then roll in. Another day chalked up for survival. Another day coming soon.

Above and Left The last generation of propeller-driven fighters appeared just as World War II was ending. The finest of these, the Grumman F8F Bearcat, could climb to 10,000 feet faster than the jets of the time. Bearcats never served the United States in combat, but some were used by the French *Armée de l'Air* in the war against the Viet Minh.

Facing The piston-engine fighters of World War II remain among the most exciting planes in the world to fly. Here a Hawker Sea Fury, the Royal Navy's last piston-engine fighter, speeds away from a North American P-51 Mustang.

Operating from British carriers in the Korean War, pilots in Sea Furies achieved notable successes against MiG-15 jets. As the major powers developed better, more reliable jets, the last piston-engine fighters continued to serve the air forces of smaller countries through the late 1950s. This Hawker Sea Fury bears the kangaroo rondel of the Royal Australian Air Force.

Jet Jockeys

All wars produce rapid, intensive growth in the efficiency of destruction, none more so than World War II. By the time it ended in 1945, you could hardly recognize it as the same affair that began with Polish cavalry striving to fend off German panzers. An entirely new weapon, the atomic bomb, altered warfare forever, and the primary means of delivering it, the airplane, became the most important vehicle of any armed force. What a change from the grudging acceptance of a few planes to scout the Western Front a mere 30 years before!

The last year of World War II saw the military debut of a new kind of flying machine. The jet engine was developed from the same concept as the turbo-supercharger, first devised in 1918 to improve high-altitude performance in piston engines. Britain's Frank Whittle, an RAF engineer and test pilot, patented his idea for jet propulsion in 1930. At first, he couldn't get the British military to pay attention. Working on with private funds, he built a prototype in 1937 which would run for half an hour. When the government looked again in 1938, they declared the engine a secret and hired the Gloster Company to build a plane around it.

Meanwhile, a young German named Hans von Ohain had been testing his own turbojet concept since 1934. Generously backed by aviation tycoon Ernst Heinkel, his team got the jet-powered Heinkel 178 airborne on August 27, 1939– five days before World War II began. Whittle finally saw his engine propel a plane, the Gloster E-28/39, on May 15, 1941.

Combat jets began to hit the skies in 1944. Again, the Germans were first with the twin-engined Messerschmitt 262. Designed as an interceptor, it began terrorizing Allied missions. It could have badly hurt the air armies of B-17s, for at well over 500 miles per hour, it was a full 100 miles per hour faster than the best Allied propeller-driven fighters, and even a tad faster than the Gloster Meteor, a jet fighter which the Brits got flying at almost the same time. But by then the Allied air forces had more planes, more supplies, and more fuel than the Germans, and their bombing missions interfered with

Facing The United States sent both jet and propeller-driven fighters into combat in Korea. Jets had the speed advantage, while prop fighters maneuvered far better at low altitudes. Navy pilots took the Vought F4U-7 Corsair (background) on ground-attack and bombing missions. Some tangled with enemy aircraft; one Marine Corsair pilot reportedly knocked down a MiG-15 jet—something pilots in the McDonnell F2H-2 Banshee (foreground) never did. Based on carriers, the Banshee performed reconnaissance and bombing missions.

Right The Bell P-59 Airacomet, first test-flown in 1942, never went into combat. With a top speed of 409 miles per hour, the P-59B couldn't have kept up with late-model propeller-driven fighters—to say nothing of the Messerschmitt Me 262. Instead, P-59s at domestic bases introduced American pilots to jet flight and gave American engineers the data to build faster planes.

Facing, above Great Britain's Gloster Meteor began flying combat sorties in the summer of 1944. By then, the RAF was well supplied with excellent prop fighters, so British pilots tested the Meteor on home defense missions, chasing down Hitler's V-1 cruise missiles as they came screaming over England. A few flew ground-attack missions on the Continent in 1945, but none crossed paths with the faster Messerschmitt Me 262.

Facing, below In the postwar period, RAF pilots like James Lomas broke European speed records with improved Gloster Meteors. Lomas flew from Edinburgh to London in half an hour one day in 1947, averaging about 600 miles per hour.

German manufacturing. And Hitler, raging over the effect of the great Allied raids, converted many Me 262s into hit-and-run bombers, a job for which they lacked range and temperament.

Where were the Yanks during this sudden explosion out of the confines of the piston engine? The U.S. Navy, trainer of some of the world's best pilots, indicated in January 1941 that its crystal ball was one of the world's cloudiest. Jets, declared Navy experts, are a lot of nonsense. The Army was more prescient. Ever alert to new ideas, Air Forces commander General Hap Arnold got a chance to see what Whittle was up to in 1941, and the Army flew a prototype of our first American jet, the Bell XP-59A Airacomet (powered by a Whittle design), in 1942.

I happened to be passing through a California air base in early 1945 when one of these was shooting landings. I heard a distant moan and saw a bulky creature slumping toward the strip on final. As its approach began to look a bit low, the pilot cracked on some throttle, and the moan rose to a banshee scream. But nothing happened to the plane. It kept sagging in short for a few long seconds until the thrust finally took hold and nudged it over the end of the runway.

The jet jockey finished his landing run, turned off, and with a thundering roar lurched around for another go around. Straightening out for takeoff, he poured on power, and a fiendish new sound, the shrill howl of the jet age, made me clap my hands over my ears. Again, the '59 just sat there like a clump of sod until the thrust inched it forward and it mushed into the air.

Above The Messerschmitt Me 262 could not turn the tide of war, but with its remarkable power and speed, it did give elite Luftwaffe pilots like Adolf Galland a fleeting taste of air warfare's future. To Galland, the Me 262's tremendous acceleration felt like "angels pushing." At war's end, special Allied teams seized Me 262s (including the one shown here) for testing and research. The plane's swept wings, configured to accommodate the weighty engine pods, would turn out to be a lasting contribution to jet design.

Right Adapted to wartime shortages, Heinkel He 162s were constructed with a minimum of strategic materials. The single jet engine was mounted on the strongest possible place—the top of the fuselage. Only 116 were completed by the war's end, and a few may have flown missions from a German base near Denmark.

"Not for me," murmured another piston-engine fighter pilot watching beside me. "But," he added, "I guess there's no torque."

That was something for us old-fashioned "reciprocaters" to think about. Jets had no torque. Our powerful piston-engine fighters badly wanted to rotate in the opposite direction from the propeller. To compensate, the rudder was set as though for a right turn. But when you started your takeoff run, your engine winding up, your 12-foot propeller wheeling full speed to the right, the rudder had little effect. It needed your muscle on the right pedal to keep the plane from wheeling to the left.

When you dove, the offset rudder worked all too well. You had to come on hard with the left pedal to keep from slewing sideways. Trim tabs helped, but I never heard of anyone using trim tabs during combat. As my fighter pilot friend Don Lopez noted in his book, *Into the Teeth of the Tiger*, you could tell an old P-40 hand by his leg muscles.

Regrettably, I never converted to jets. Those friends who did reported that they were smooth, quiet, and easy. They'd roll with ailerons alone. They were fun to fly. But unfortunately, those screaming turbines sometimes threw a blade or quit and blew up, and that was all she wrote. One acquaintance from New Guinea who bought the farm

Jet fighters first met in aerial combat in Korea. The Lockheed F-80 Shooting Star, the United States' first operational jet fighter, faced the MiG-15—a newer plane with a speed advantage of 70 miles per hour. Still, credit for the first jet victory over another jet went to USAF Lieutenant Russell Brown, who sent down a Chinese MiG-15 on November 8, 1950. As faster F-86 Sabres began to reach the front line, F-80s (including the one shown here) shifted from interception to ground-attack missions.

Above The only fighter ever designed and built in Canada, the Canadian Avro CF-100 served the RCAF for 30 years, starting as a frontline fighter in Canada and in NATO posts in Europe, and ending as a trainer. Although Canadian fighter pilots liked to call it "the Clunk," the CF-100 was a highly reliable, competitive fighter.

Facing The Lockheed T-33 trainer was a two-seat version of the F-80 Shooting Star. Introduced in 1948, it served in the U.S. Air Force for a decade. Rolls-Royce Nene engines made the license-built Canadian version faster than its American counterpart, and RCAF fighter pilots still trained in the "T-bird" in the 1980s.

testing a P-80, Lockheed's sleek Shooting Star, was Dick Bong.

In the last days of World War II, the Luftwaffe flung another oddball fighter up at the huge B-17 fleets. This was the little Me 163, armed with a pair of cannons and powered by a rocket. The Germans called it the Komet. Though it only carried fuel enough for one pass and then a dead-stick landing, the American bomber boys hated it. One of them told me what it was like to be attacked by an Me 163:

There we were, churning along over Germany, when this little thing came straight up at us, so fast no one had time to call it in. It passed between my plane and the leader, firing all the way, then ran out of fuel and dove straight down through the same gap, guns blazing, bullets flying all around. No one laid a glove on it. When it was gone, I saw the copilot of the lead plane wave a big white handkerchief up and down in his window. Total, unconditional surrender! That was how we all felt.

The Komet was too little, too late, but it was the shape of other things to come.

That same rocket concept would break the so-called "sound barrier." World War II fighter pilots ran into a problem we called "compressibility": indicating close to 500 miles per hour in a dive, planes became unmanageable. Controls stiffened as though locked. The plane would buffet dangerously and tend to "tuck under," to go past the perpendicular. Pulling out was very hard until the dive slowed in the friction of thicker air. It seemed that the nearer you came to the speed of sound (700 miles per hour at 43,000 feet), the heavier the stress on your ship.

RAF engineers got a late-model Spitfire closer to the speed of sound than any other reciprocating engine fighter, and realized that the thin, graceful wing had a lot to do with this performance. High-speed wings came off the drawing boards, and with the kick of liquid-fuel rockets, Bell's cylindrical X-1, flown by ex-fighter Chuck Yeager, was dropped by a B-29 at 20,000 feet on an October day in 1947. The bright bullet, named Glamorous Glennis for Yeager's wife, slipped past Mach 1, the speed of sound, with barely a flutter.

The "barrier" ghost was laid to rest. Compressibility had been created by the structure of propeller-driven planes. Their whirling blades lost efficiency at high speed. Getting their thick wings through the build-up of air was like cutting a stick of butter with the handle of a knife instead of the blade.

Eager to explore the new supersonic realm came the new jet fighters, with swept wings, snub noses enclosing air intakes, thundering tail pipes, and bubble canopies

Above When work on the de Havilland Vampire began in 1941, turbojets had little thrust. To maximize thrust in the Vampire, de Havilland made the fuselage very short, reconfiguring the tail on twin booms. Vampires flew in RAF frontline squadrons from 1946 to 1957, and in the air forces of smaller countries as late as 1980.

Facing In the late 1940s, Britain jeopardized its leading position in aviation as the government drastically reduced military commitments and expenditures. While riskier, more advanced supersonic designs were delayed, the subsonic de Havilland Venom, a direct successor of the Vampire, went into production. Top speed in the Vampire was 548 miles per hour; the heavier, more powerful Venom inched over the 600-mile-per-hour mark, and saw combat over the Suez in 1956.

perched forward to offer a picture-window view. When the Korean War began in 1950, jet fighters began meeting each other in combat.

The pilots who flew F-86s and MiG 15s over the mountains of Korea were a mixed lot. Most American squadron and flight leaders were veterans of the earlier war, called back as reservists. Slightly balding, gray around the ears, they'd gotten used to fretting over which kid had left his bicycle in the driveway. Now they were asked to recapture the dash, the joy of action, the controlled recklessness of their youth.

I recall reading an account in *Life* of a high-ranking fighter pilot and World War II veteran who had battled, bailed out, and been rescued in Korea. And with a rush of memories, I realized that this man had been my squadron operations officer when I first joined it early in 1943. Another old vet, Frank Gabreski, who'd clobbered 28 German planes over Europe in the forties, upped his score in Korea.

With the old tigers fought jet-age youngsters, their training so good that it almost made up for their lack of experience. They were chosen as fighter pilots for many more reasons than the old World War II qualification (actually used in my time) that they be no taller than five feet ten.

Their reactions had to be faster than ever; their judgment absolutely faultless; their decisions instant and 100 percent correct. Flying close to Mach 1, they had to see and identify an enemy plane at the farthest range of vision, figure out what to do, and do it, all within the blink of an eye. After all, they were moving at close to the speed of a bullet.

The United States Air Force had finally become what Billy Mitchell and Hap Arnold wanted it to be, an independent service, in 1947, and Korea gave the new USAF a chance to show its stuff as its F-86 Sabres duelled with the very similar MiG-15s. The fighter jocks developed combat formation techniques that paid off handsomely. Speed was now too high for more than four planes to fly a squadron mission. The planes spread wide enough to keep four pairs of eyes always searching the sky, yet close enough for wingmen to read their leaders' large squadron numbers. Those wingmen dropped back a bit in attack, so their guns could bear on the target. They crossed under their leaders when necessary to keep the whole sky under close surveillance. It was how we tried to fly in World War II, but better taught and better learned.

MiG pilots were generally less aggressive than the Americans, but their planes could fly about 4,000 feet higher than our F-86s. Combats were brief: sight the enemy, climb and turn toward him, hit, run, break back up toward the sun, and hit again if

Above and Facing Expatriate German engineers and captured German engines helped the Soviet Union launch its first jet fighters. But the biggest boost came in 1946, when Britain licensed a Soviet version of the best jet engine of the time, the Rolls-Royce Nene. Powered by the Nene, Mikoyan and Gurevich's highly successful MiG-15 was virtually equal to any jet fighter it met in Korea.

Above Simple by today's standards, the cockpit of this North American F-86 Sabre shows the ergonomic advances that jet fighting demanded. Increased speeds meant that decisions had to be made faster than ever: instruments had to be instantly legible, controls more responsive. Higher G-forces mandated better cushioning. Pilots also wore pressure suits to keep blood flowing to their eyes and brains. High-G maneuvers are physically punishing, and jets burn fuel very fast, so missions became much shorter, averaging 90 minutes—Pacific patrols of World War II could be as long as 10 hours.

Facing When the F-86 arrived in Korea, United Nations forces regained air superiority over the Communists' MiG-15s. MiGs flew a bit higher, but with superior tactics and training, American pilots in F-86s came away with a victory ratio of 10:1.

169

Above The Republic F-84F Thunderstreak, a contemporary of the F-86, could be coaxed for short periods to speeds just under Mach 1. Earlier variants of the F-84 had straight wings; swept wings and a more powerful engine boosted the Thunderstreak's top speed by about 60 miles per hour. Its designer, Alexander Kartveli, had already built two noteworthy fighters, the trim-looking Seversky P-35 monoplane of 1935 and the famous P-47 Thunderbolt.

Right Radar for night fighting nestles within the black nose cone of this North American F-86D, an all-weather, rocket-equipped variant of the Sabre. The jet's air intake has been shifted to a chin scoop under the nose. Practicality dictated the silvery look of Sabres and other early jets; traditional paint jobs could cut maximum speed by as much as 20 miles per hour.

possible. Aces were hard to come by, but since the folks back home required some heroes, the best (and luckiest) of the F-86 pilots were given every chance to score.

James Jabara was first to pass the magic five mark, and was shipped home to boost morale. In early 1953, with more targets in "MiG Alley," a heavily contested air corridor over North Korea, Jabara came back for more, got nine in eight weeks, and ended up as one of the war's top scorers.

The war's leading ace was Joseph "Mac" McConnell, who seemed intent on showing his buddies what a former navigator could do. Once when he was downed by flak and picked out of the sea, he flew again the next day. His final score: 16. But individual tallies didn't mean as much as general performance. The Americans shot down an average of a baker's dozen MiGs for every Sabre lost.

The Korean War was the last major conflict in which guns were used in airplanes. Combat there proved that a pilot flying at sonic speed needed a weapon that could hit the target at the moment he knew it existed. And he needed to know it existed before he could see it. Science had the answers: miniaturized and sophisticated detectors and homing missiles.

Above Five months in 1953 was all it took for Joseph McConnell to shoot down 16 MiGs from his F-86, making him the top American ace in the Korean War. Learning the ways of the jet fighter, American squadrons shifted from large World War II-style formations to the "fluid four"—two pairs of leaders and wings, trading attack and back-up roles.

Left The Italian markings on this F-84 testify to the Thunderstreak's long reign as a frontline fighter around the world. Like the F-86 Sabre, the Thunderstreak straddled two very different generations—its jet engines and swept wings foreshadowed fighters ever since, but its weapons were among the last to be aimed entirely by the pilot.

One Navy pilot described the catapult-assisted launch of early Navy jet fighters as "a deadly serious ballet-drama." The slow acceleration of 1940s turbojet engines meant that fighter jets required as much as a mile and a half to take off on land. To get airborne from a carrier, the same aircraft had to be revved to 100 percent thrust, then hurled by catapult to 115 miles per hour within 100 feet. The Navy liked the Air Force's swept-wing Furies and Sabres from the start, but had to wait till 1952 to accommodate the faster planes on carriers. F9F-6 Cougars, shown here preparing to launch from USS *Yorktown* in 1953 or 1954, were swept-wing variants of the proven F9F Panther.

Above The Navy version of the famous swept-wing Sabre was the FJ-3 Fury. Here the most numerous variant, the FJ-3D, completes a landing on board USS *Lexington*. These Furies were among the first to carry early versions of the heat-seeking Sidewinder missile, a weapon destined to change the nature of air combat.

Left Seaplanes and flying boats had been part of the Navy's inventory since Glenn Curtiss delivered the Navy's first aircraft, the A-1 floatplane, in 1911. That tradition was nearing its end in the 1950s, but Convair tried to keep it going with the Seadart, a supersonic fighter designed to take off and land in sheltered waters. Five Convair XF2Y Seadarts were built for testing, and three of these were flown extensively in tests from 1952 to 1957, when the program was cancelled.

173

Above The Lockheed F-104 Starfighter, the first operational fighter to exceed Mach 2, was one of many firsts for Clarence L. "Kelly" Johnson and his design team. Their first success had been the P-38, which brought Lockheed into military aviation. Then came the F-80, the first operational American jet fighter, which went from sketches to prototypes in less than six months. In the 1960s, Johnson's team would build the SR-71 Blackbird reconnaissance plane, the world's fastest operational military aircraft, which flew at Mach 3.

Right Just as the early jet fighters of the United States, Great Britain, and France have had extended service lives in smaller countries, Soviet types from the MiG-15 on continue to fly in the air forces of their present and former allies. These Albanian fighter pilots of 1964 are scrambling for their MiG-17s, purchased from Moscow in the 1950s. More recently, Albania has received its planes from Communist China's state aircraft factory, which continues to churn out copies of 1950s MiG designs.

Above and Left Intended as a replacement for the Gloster Meteor, Sydney Camm's Hawker Hunter gained a reputation as one of the finest subsonic jet fighters ever built. As the RAF shifted to supersonic fighters in the 1960s, large numbers of Hunters were reconditioned and sold to other countries, where they continued to fly in the 1980s. During the Six-Day War of 1967, Iraqi pilots in Hunters scored some of the Arab alliance's only successes against the Israeli air force. The trainer variant of the Hawker Hunter, the T.7 (left), has a wider two-seat cockpit.

Overleaf The Convair F-106 Delta Dart has been a pilot's favorite, a fast, rock-solid, long-range flyer, for over a quarter century. Introduced in 1960 to counter the threat of a nuclear attack by supersonic Soviet bombers, the Delta Dart cruises near Mach 2, and its fire-control system works with ground-based radar to guide aircraft and weapons toward the target. The delta wing gives the F-106 both stability and low drag for Mach 2 flight. A delta wing's leading edges can be angled more sharply than a swept wing's, reducing drag without sacrificing control surfaces along the trailing edge.

Above and Facing The designers of the English Electric Lightning, Britain's first great supersonic fighter, wanted the low drag of the delta wing and the added control of separate tail surfaces. Part of the solution was a delta-like wing, swept back 60 degrees, with a triangular excision where the trailing edge and fuselage meet. The plane's equally unique fuselage, with its vertically stacked engines and tailpipes, enabled the designers to combine the thrust of two jet engines without widening the fuselage and increasing drag. An electronic weapons system guided the Lightning toward targets and helped aim its rockets. Replacing the Hawker Hunter, the aircraft served frontline RAF squadrons until the early 1980s.

Right Sweden's jet fighters, built by Saab, are fully competitive with the productions of far larger, wealthier countries. Prototypes of the supersonic Draken began flying in 1955. Equipped with advanced radar fire-control systems, the most numerous variant, the J35F, provided frontline defense from the early 1960s to the early 1980s.

THE AGE OF THE SUPERSONIC FIGHTER

Once they'd tasted supersonic speed, the world's air forces quickly became addicted. The Cold War inspired swept-wing and delta-wing fighters that routinely passed Mach 1 and even Mach 2. The "Century" series of American fighters, the F-100, F-101, F-102, F-104, F-105, and F-106, exemplified the trend. The F-104 could go well over Mach 2, thanks to its stubby little wings—"fins," if you prefer—with a span of only 21 feet, 11 inches, and leading edges so sharp that ground crews sheathed them to avoid cuts. Russia answered with new MiG-19s and MiG-23s, and the rest of Europe joined the race with Mirages, Mystères, Saabs, and other sleek designs. All were affected by the Cold War dictum: bombers flying fast and high must deliver the nukes; supersonic fighters, bristling with electronic missiles, refueled by tankers, must protect them.

In theory, the U.S. fighter pilot of the late 1960s was so thoroughly equipped to knock down enemy planes at long range and high speed that only the most foolhardy Russian or Chinese pilot would even think of crossing his path. As a hypothetical mission begins, he meets his "backseater"—the radar and intercept officer, who is also a pilot—on a carrier flight deck. They climb into their big F-4B Phantom II, trundle over to the catapult, and, at a signal, they're zapped into the air: 150 knots from a standstill in a couple of seconds. They climb to the edge of the stratosphere in no time flat and tool along at Mach 1.3 or so.

The backseater picks up a bogey on radar. The air-to-air missile system "acquires" it—in other words, locks on. A heat-seeking Sidewinder flies up the enemy's tail pipe and blows him to bits. Hooray for our side!

Then came the realities of actual war. Fighter pilots learned that supersonic flight burned fuel at an outrageous rate and made identification of targets almost impossible. Enemy radar glommed onto you unless you hit the deck. Your heat-seeking

Above The gun camera records the moment when a Republic F-105 Thunderchief's 20mm cannon hits the wing of a North Vietnamese MiG-17. The MiG had reportedly bounced F-105s in formation, but didn't succeed in taking advantage of its surprise attack. American pilots more commonly scored with one of two guided missiles, the heat-seeking Sidewinder and the radar-seeking Sparrow. Of these, the simpler Sidewinder was markedly more successful; one in five reached the target, while only one in nine Sparrows did. New versions of both continue to arm fighters around the world.

Facing The McDonnell F-4 Phantom II is the most significant American fighter since World War II. When Americans began flying air combat missions in Vietnam in 1965, the second-generation Phantoms, the Navy's F-4B and the Air Force's F-4C, had just begun to reach the squadrons. When air combat stopped in 1973, Phantoms had scored 72 percent of all victories over North Vietnamese aircraft. With that record came many costly lessons about the nature of supersonic combat and the use of guided weaponry.

missiles might home in on the sun or a friendly plane or a warm spot on the ground. Also, that bogey was apt to shoot back.

When that happened, you might try firing off a hot magnesium flare to draw the enemy missile or spraying metallic chaff to confuse his radar. Never mind speed. You now needed to wrench your plane around, to make like the Red Baron. These were the "high-G maneuvers" the Air Force and Navy talk about, when the big jets twisted and turned so violently that their pilots were all but crushed in their cockpits, oxygen masks sagging, lips drawn down, eyes popping from sunken cheeks.

The Middle East, a perpetual hot spot, exploded into the Six-Day War in 1967, and the superbly trained and equipped Israeli Air Force made short work of its Egyptian and Syrian opponents. But the Israeli fighter pilots, perhaps to their own surprise, scored mostly in good old-fashioned dogfights, squirreling their heavy Mirage IIIs around at low altitudes, getting most of their kills with plain old gunfire.

This ancient tactic was practiced long after the Six-Day War ended. Top Israeli ace Asher Snir wrote of attacking a single outdated MiG-17 in a 1970 border incident and being led into a rat race down among the barren hills where his ultramodern jet did not belong. "This is not what I had taught others. One must not fly at such levels

Above The MiG-21, the first Soviet fighter capable of Mach 2 flight, appeared in 1956. Thirty-five years later, a few still fly in the Soviet Air Force, and many more can be found in Soviet-supplied air forces around the world. Intelligence reports had estimated its capabilities quite highly, but the MiG-21 suffered from the same faults as the first Western Mach 2 fighters. Designed as an interceptor loaded with sophisticated radar-guided weaponry, it was only marginally more suited to "turn-and-burn, yank-and-bank" jet dogfighting than the F-4 Phantom. As American pilots relearned the basics of tactical aviation, the MiG threat diminished. By the 1973 cease-fire, MiGs had accounted for only seven percent of all American airplanes lost in Vietnam.

Facing From 1965 to 1968, 75 percent of the U.S. Air Force's assault missions over North Vietnam were carried out in the Republic F-105 Thunderchief. Nicknamed the "Thud," this supersonic fighter-bomber carried over six tons of weaponry and cruised at Mach 2. Like other American supersonic designs from the fifties, the Thunderchief had a "coke-bottle" fuselage, narrowing toward the center, then widening again. This shape, devised at the National Advisory Committee for Aeronautics (NACA), helped minimize drag as the plane accelerated to supersonic speed.

of risk that only success separates them from recklessness. But something told me...that today and with this man this was the only way."

Snir dimly recalls ground obstacles, long minutes of passes and pull-outs, missed shots, an occasional buzz when his missile "saw" its target. He knew better than to waste his Sidewinder on a shot that would sag into the ground just below. But at last, drenched with sweat, he caught the MiG crossing a wide valley and the missile had room to sink and then home in.

"The last second of the brave and talented man's life is still etched in my memory: the missile with its thin smoke plume hiding beneath the wing, the large orange flash..."

Similarly, in Vietnam, Americans pitted all their hottest fighters against enemy MiGs and quickly learned that real missions have little to do with theory. Two planes, the F-4 Phantom II and the F-105 Thunderchief (known as the "Thud"), carried out most combat missions against the MiG-17, MiG-19, and MiG-21, and this time, the Americans didn't do too well.

In *The Ace Factor*, Mike Spick points out that the Phantom was so big that it could be seen before its pilot saw the enemy. A more basic problem, he says, was the lack of training given to American fighter pilots in air combat. Supersonic flight and sophisticated armament they knew. But the young air warriors hadn't learned to squirm around the sky at low level in millions of bucks' worth of thundering hardware designed

Above By some estimates, over 8,000 MiG-21s were manufactured after 1956, making it the most numerous supersonic fighter in the world. In the hands of a first-rate pilot, it was always a match for Americans in F-4s and Israelis in French Dassault Mirages. Both in North Vietnam and the Middle East, however, Soviet-trained pilots had far fewer precombat flight hours than their opponents.

Left At the start of the American air war in Vietnam, the North Vietnamese Air Force possessed 53 MiG-15s and MiG-17s and very few experienced fighter pilots. With the help of Soviet instructors like the man in the center of this group of NVAF cadets, competent flyers quickly emerged.

Facing During the first period of air combat in Vietnam, from 1965 to 1968, pilots in the Navy's Vought F-8 Crusader compiled the best victory ratio of any aircraft in the war: six downed enemy aircraft for each Crusader lost. Navy pilots attributed their successes in the "MiG Master" to the fact that during the late fifties and early sixties, Crusader squadrons continued to practice gunnery and dogfighting.

The McDonnell F-4 Phantom's two-seater configuration complicated the business of ranking aces in Vietnam. Navy pilot Randall Cunningham (right) and radar intercept officer William Driscoll (left) were the war's only ace team. Three USAF flyers also became aces. Two of them, Steve Ritchie and Charles DeBellevue, scored four victories together and one each with other partners. Geoffrey Feinstein achieved his five kills as radar intercept officer with four different pilots. Later an instructor at the Navy Fighter Weapons School (Topgun), Cunningham came up with the program's motto: "You fight as well as you train."

for high-altitude speed, armed with missiles more apt to hit mountains than MiGs.

However, Americans are naturally pretty good fighter pilot material and soon learned the new realities of limited war. Flying in elements, their planes at least half a mile and perhaps several miles apart, they learned to skim the ground beneath the radar's sweep, utilizing a handy mountain line ("Thud Ridge" was one), refueling when they had to from the trailing hose of a flying tanker. They learned to cope with the scary SAMs, the Russian ground-to-air missiles that were their worst foe. A good pilot would climb when he saw the smoke of a SAM, then dive more suddenly than the SAM could.

Eventually the strange rigors of Vietnam forged many good Air Force and Navy fighter pilots. The Army produced its own new breed, the helicopter pilot, a match for anyone in skill and guts. Individual names didn't mean much because most Air Force and Navy fighters flew the Phantom, a two-man plane. The Navy's Randall Cunningham and William Driscoll got three MiGs in one day. The Air Force tried to come up with aces of its own, but had to be content with forging mere heroes and many leaders.

The Air Force's Daniel "Chappie" James, a Phantom II pilot, led his flight on a fighter sweep that copped seven MiGs. Chappie upheld the tradition of excellence set by World War II's first black fighter group, the famous 332nd, which he'd joined as a youngster without seeing action. He got plenty in Korea. And his Vietnam record made him a general. That happened to other Phantom II drivers, such as Dick Pascoe and Bill

Above Daniel "Chappie" James was deputy commander of Colonel Robin Olds' Tactical Fighter Wing. From their base at Ubon, Thailand, he flew 78 combat missions over Vietnam. James was big for a fighter pilot—6'4" and 220 pounds—and when asked how he fit in the F-4's cockpit, reportedly said, "I don't get into it. I put it on." James became the United States' first black four-star general in 1975.

Left North Vietnamese flight commanders like Pham Ngok Lan had to contend with shortages of fuel, a limited supply of airplanes, and inexperienced pilots. But the North also had certain advantages. By 1967, most North Vietnamese air space was well covered with radar, and MiG pilots had plenty of warning when U.S Air Force or Navy planes approached. As the Americans approached Hanoi, they were flying over ever-deadlier concentrations of AAA and SAM installations. The Americans repeatedly flew the same routes, often at the same time of day. Finally, Americans fought under "Rules of Engagement" and highly detailed mission orders which limited their tactics. They seldom bombed airfields or parked aircraft. They could not bomb a SAM site until it was completed. And they could not fly within 30 miles of the Chinese border, giving MiGs an easy escape route.

As the red star on the intake spiller plate below each cockpit shows, pilot-backseater teams in each of these McDonnell F-4 Phantoms shot down a MiG in North Vietnam. Phantoms were invaluable from the start of the American air effort. F-4Bs flew the Navy's first raid against North Vietnam. F-4Cs got the war's (and the Air Force's) first combat kills, 2 MiG-17s on July 10, 1965. The Navy followed with two on July 17. But it wasn't always easy. As Navy pilot John Nichols later wrote, Phantom drivers weren't ready at first for the reality of MiG combat, a "tangle with nimble dogfighters eyeball to eyeball down in the weeds."

Above Colonel Robin Olds commanded the 8th Tactical Fighter Wing for a year in 1966 and 1967. In that period, the 8th shot down more MiGs than any other tactical unit. Olds was fortunate to be under the command of William Momyer, a hands-on Air Force general who trusted fighter pilots' assessments of the problems with the air war. The plan for Operation Bolo, in which Olds' unit mimicked the flight characteristics of F-105 Thunderchiefs in their F-4s, deceiving a MiG patrol and destroying seven of them, originated with General Momyer.

Right The United States Air Force Museum in Dayton, Ohio, displays the McDonnell F-4C Phantom II in which Colonel Olds and his RIO, Lieutenant Stephen B. Crocker, shot down two MiGs in one day.

Facing Grumman F-14 Tomcats reached the U.S. Navy's carrier squadrons as the Vietnam War was winding down. A second-generation supersonic interceptor, the two-seat, twin-engine F-14 is designed to be effective in a very wide range of combat situations. The variable-geometry wings are computer-controlled and adjust automatically to the flying situation: fully forward for slower maneuvering, fully back in a delta shape for cruising at Mach 2, or anywhere in between.

Kirk. Best remembered of all is Robin Olds.

He'd made ace in World War II, and by the 1960s, he was a full colonel, commanding the Eighth Tactical Fighter Wing. Noting the problems with missiles, he helped convince the Pentagon to put guns back in the fighters. Then his gang could fight. He liked to plan sting operations. Once he sent his F-4s off, low and slow, trying to look like Thuds loaded down with bombs for a tactical strike. The MiGs bit, howling down to attack. And the Phantoms dropped their wing tanks, poured on the coal, and suddenly turned lethal again.

On one such well-planned fighter sweep, Olds led his lads into a blistering soirée with MiG-21s. They got seven in 12 minutes without losing a plane. Olds managed the affair, aware of everything that was going on around him. He was like that, always totally in charge, always aggressive.

Leadership came first with Olds, and he missed being an ace by one victory. It could have come a number of times, but Olds wouldn't lead his flight into a nontarget area, needlessly risking SAMs and heavy flak just because some MiGs were stooging around waiting to get clobbered. To him, a mission was serious business, not an ego trip.

Olds made general. More than that, he was acknowledged the best fighter pilot in Vietnam. You can look at his plane in the Air Force Museum in Dayton, Ohio.

What changes Robin Olds saw in his career! From the blur of propeller blades to the hot blue pencil of jet thrust, from compressibility to the sonic boom, from the snarl

Drawing on Navy flyers' experiences in Vietnam, the designers of the F-14 gave it the speed of an interceptor and the maneuverability of a close-range fighter. Robin Olds once said, "The guy you don't see will kill you," and the F-14 does everything it can to keep that from happening. With its bubble canopy, it was the first supersonic fighter to give the pilot a 360-degree field of vision. Three types of guided missiles, the Phoenix, the Sidewinder, and the Sparrow, work through a fire-control system that can (in theory) shoot at six targets simultaneously while tracking eighteen others. The Tomcat's radar will pick up fighter-size targets 100 miles away, and an electronically magnified TV camera in the nose enables the pilot to "see" targets 10 miles away. A 20mm cannon can be fired against close-range targets.

Contemporary American combat aircraft are painted in neutral greys and blues that blend with both the sky and the earth. Here the four most recent U.S. Air Force fighters fly in formation (top to bottom): the McDonnell Douglas F-15, McDonnell F-4 Phantom, McDonnell Douglas F/A-18, and General Dynamics F-16.

of his P-38 to the howl of his F-4.

Olds wasn't the only World War II veteran still flying a generation later. But by the end of the Vietnam War, most old-timers had been pried out of the cockpit and stuck behind a desk. A sad letdown? Not for the country. At last, combat-tested fighter pilots moved into positions of some authority at the Pentagon. Their influence was felt as purchasing policy veered away from supersonic interceptors and back to fighters— fast and sophisticated, but also agile enough to fight. Result: the F-14, F-15, F-16, and F/A-18.

Grumman designed the F-14 Tomcat for the U.S. Navy: a big carrier plane with a swing wing which reflected the theory that planes should fulfill a variety of missions. The similar U.S. Air Force F-15, built by McDonnell Douglas, followed. Then General Dynamics produced the F-16 (the one with a single rudder) for the Air Force. It was smaller, lighter, more maneuverable, and could only be controlled with the help of

computers. In other words, it was a "fly-by-wire" plane. So was the Navy's F/A-18, slightly larger than the F-16, but breathtakingly maneuverable, as the Navy's Blue Angels demonstrate in their air shows.

Built with space-age materials, the F-16 and F/A-18 are light, strong, and impressive to watch when put through their paces. You see them at air shows and on Armed Forces Day. One will taxi out on a runway—a dainty little craft that seems harmless enough until it takes off. Then it stands on its tail and simply bores straight up through city smog and distant cirrostratus, up out of sight to where the French children are sure that the immortal Guynemer still flies.

The great thunder of the engines diminishes to a faint mutter. Then down comes the fighter in a softly whistling descent, pausing to barrel-roll, to "cut the cake," to scream up into a tight loop or a twisting Immelman. And then, at ground level, the little lady proceeds to turn inside the perimeter of the airfield, pirouetting as though she were a

Ambitious ideas marked the design and procurement of the General Dynamics F-111, a multipurpose tactical fighter/bomber intended to replace the "Century Series." It was the first aircraft to have variable-geometry swing wings, and the first to have terrain-following radar (TFR), which automatically guides the plane over terrain at altitudes too low for most enemy radar and missiles. Defense Secretary Robert McNamara pushed the F-111 as a money-saver which both the Air Force and Navy could use. But after a long, expensive, and troublesome test period, the Navy rejected the F-111 and ordered the Grumman F-14. The Air Force cut back its orders sharply, using the F-111 mainly as a strategic bomber.

Above Steam from the carrier's bow catapults envelops an aircraft taxi director, or "Yellow Shirt," as he directs a McDonnell Douglas F/A-18 Hornet clear of the landing area. The U.S. Navy ordered the F/A-18 in the late 1970s as a lightweight, multimission replacement for the F-4.

Facing General Dynamics followed the disappointing F-111 with the remarkable F-16 Fighting Falcon, the "Electric Jet." Maneuverability guided the F-16's design. Its strong, light, carbon-epoxy frame can withstand 9 Gs (about all a pressure-suited pilot can stand), and computerized "fly-by-wire" controls maximize the F-16's inherently unstable flight characteristics. A side-arm control mounted on an arm rest helps the pilot keep hold of the stick under high Gs, and head-up instrumentation enables him to keep his eyes on the target.

1912 Curtiss showing off over a race track. Nose high and throttle back, she drags over the field at a speed so slow that I, for one, shudder at the loss of flyability. But when power comes on, the plane accelerates contemptuously, seeking the heights again at blistering speed.

These are modern fighters, all proving that high-G turns and sudden climbs and dives, skids and slips, the aerial unpredictability that saves a pilot's neck—all these are still needed.

Above The airframe of the Israeli-built Kfir is derived from the Dassault Mirage V, and the engine is the General Electric J79 turbojet, which was also used in the McDonnell F-4. When the Israeli Air Force defeated the Syrians over the Bekáa Valley in 1982, Kfir pilots scored three victories over the MiGs, while F-15 and F-16 pilots destroyed over 80 Syrian aircraft.

Facing Two Douglas A-4 Skyhawks and a General Dynamics F-16 Fighting Falcon pass over Key West, Florida. The Soviet stars on their tails mark them as aggressors in simulated combat exercises. To military budget-watchers, the use of multimillion-dollar aircraft in high-risk combat games is a nightmare; to fighter pilots, mindful of their unpreparedness in Vietnam, it is the best way to ensure combat readiness.

Right Fighting alongside more expensive, powerful, and heavily armed McDonnell F-15s in the Bekáa Valley, General Dynamics F-16s proved that light, highly maneuverable fighters remain a necessity. F-16 pilots made the most of close-combat situations, scoring 44 kills, while F-15 pilots used their planes' multitarget fire-control systems to engage at longer ranges and shoot down 40 Syrian planes.

Facing Saab continued its line of capable fighters for the Swedish Air Force with the Viggen, a Mach 2 multirole aircraft. Two versions exist; the AJ37 of 1971 is an attack plane, and the faster JA37 of 1979 is primarily an interceptor.

Above The Mitsubishi F-1 is the first fighter to be built in Japan since the end of World War II. Based upon the Mitsubishi T-2 trainer, Japan's first supersonic aircraft, the F-1 is a light, short-range, close-support fighter, armed with a 20mm cannon and capable of carrying air-to-air missiles.

Right Mitsubishi adapted both its supersonic planes from the Northrop F-5 Tiger—the plane Japan's Self-Defense Force would probably have purchased if it hadn't chosen to build one domestically. The F-5 series, which reached air forces in 1974, was planned as a low-cost supersonic fighter for NATO countries and other U.S. allies. The F-5F two-seat version shown is a trainer built under license in Canada. F-5E Tiger IIs are flown as aggressor aircraft in American fighter training programs, simulating the MiG-21.

Facing The Hawker Siddeley Harrier was the first operational fixed-wing, vertical takeoff and landing (VTOL) military aircraft. Its four rotating nozzles can be set to vent exhaust downwards, lifting the plane straight off carrier decks or constricted fields. Rotated back to the horizontal plane, they propel the Harrier forward.

Right The delta-wing Mirage III, flying here in Swiss colors, was Dassault's entry among the Mach 2, high-altitude interceptors of the 1960s. Besides equipping their own air force, the French sold hundreds to 20 other countries. The Mirage III won particular notice in the Six-Day War of 1967 and the Yom Kippur War of 1973, when Israeli pilots came away with victory ratios of better than 10:1 against the Arab alliance.

Above Dassault achieved greater maneuverability in the Mirage F.1 by substituting a wing-and-tail configuration for the delta wing.

Facing The Mirage 2000 weighs one-third less than earlier Mirages, and a refined delta wing provides the agility required of the newest supersonic close-combat fighters.

Page 208 The Sukhoi Su-27 shows the influence of the McDonnell Douglas F-15 upon recent Soviet design. Like the F-15, the Su-27 carries advanced weapons guidance systems and can fire at targets beyond the pilot's visual range.

Page 209 Now being replaced by Sukhoi Su-27s and MiG-29s, the MiG-23, introduced in 1970, remains the most numerous Soviet frontline fighter. The MiG-23's pilot adjusts the variable-sweep wing with manual controls, choosing one of three possible angles.

Above Not all new jet fighters need be supersonic. The subsonic Aeritalia/Aermacchi/Embraer AMX, built by Italian and Brazilian companies, is designed to fly low and fast, avoiding radar and providing ground support.

Right and Facing To cope with the crushing expense of developing a new fighter/strike plane for the 1980s and 1990s, six companies from Great Britain, West Germany, and Italy teamed up on the airframe and engine of the Panavia Tornado. A NATO agency coordinates their work. Variable-sweep wings, advanced avionics, and top speed over Mach 2 make the Tornado competitive with leading Soviet and American fighters. It replaces the McDonnell Phantom F-4 in Britain and the Lockheed F-104 Starfighter in Germany and Italy.

The single-seat McDonnell F/A-18 Hornet is smaller, lighter, and less expensive to build and maintain than the twin-seat Grumman F-14 Tomcat, the U.S. Navy's other frontline fighter. Improving on the versatility of its predecessor, the F-4 Phantom, the Hornet can be converted from fighter-intercept to ground-attack mode (or vice versa) in about an hour. The catapult that launches the plane from a carrier deck takes it from 0 to 160 miles per hour in about a second.

Above The F/A-18's center of gravity lies well aft of the cockpit, a characteristic shared by the United States' other current fighters. This enables a plane to hold a very high angle of attack, but it also makes it impossible to control without computer assistance.

Facing Two General Electric J404 engines contribute to the reliability of the F/A-18. These engines do not generate as much thrust as an F-15's Pratt & Whitneys, but they have fewer moving parts and require less maintenance. The air intake on an F-15 adjusts above Mach 2 to prevent shock waves from shutting down the engine. With a maximum speed below Mach 2, the F/A-18 does not require the added complexity of the variable-geometry inlet.

Above, Left, and Facing The MiG-29 resembles the Sukhoi Su-27 in many ways, but is significantly smaller and lighter, and has a much better sustained turn rate than earlier Soviet jet fighters. The Su-27 is the Soviets' premier multirole, air-superiority giant; the MiG-29 is a more affordable strike, intercept, and close-combat fighter. Cost- and maintenance-saving measures include hydraulic rather than fly-by-wire controls and a lack of in-flight refueling gear.

Above and Facing The McDonnell Douglas F-15 Eagle has succeeded the F-4 as the United States' frontline, multirole, air-superiority fighter. A maximum speed of Mach 2.5 makes the F-15 the fastest operational fighter in the world. Once in combat, where speeds above Mach 1.2 are rare, the F-15 relies on a thrust ratio of better than 1:1 to keep up speed in the turns. Loaded with the most advanced avionics, the F-15 features the pulse-Doppler radar system for detecting enemy aircraft. Pulse-Doppler is less easily detectable than earlier warning systems and clearly discerns enemy aircraft against ground clutter at lower altitudes. Single-seat versions have been operational since 1976 and the two-seat F-15E since 1986.

218

Dassault-Breguet continues its line of delta-wing fighters with the Rafale, a light Mach 2 plane with a full array of avionics, guided missiles, and cannon. The Rafale's capabilities reflect the now-established doctrine that however fast a fighter goes, it must be able to maneuver smartly in the subsonic and Mach 1 range. Improving on the Mirage 2000, the Rafale has a canard wing aft of the cockpit, enabling it to maneuver aggressively near ground level at speeds as low as 100 miles per hour. The plane excels in maneuvers around Mach 1—the normal combat range—and can take off and land on relatively short fields, suiting it to carrier operations and concealed revetments. Using an innovative voice-command system, the pilot speaks to the plane to control the radio, get systems updates, and arm weapons. Where a miscue could be fatal—firing weapons and lowering landing gear—the pilot still uses manual control.

FIGHTER PILOTS: THE FUTURE

My squadron meets for reunions—a gathering of nice old gentlemen, all the same height, all wondering if they really did the things they half remember—and we sometimes mention the imminent extinction of our breed. We can only shrug, of course, and admire the breathtaking shows of the Thunderbirds and Blue Angels. We had our time at it, long ago. And, as one old friend said, "We're lucky we lived through it, and luckier still that we *did* it."

Sometimes we talk about the X-29, one of the test designs that look to the future of the fighter plane. You can see a full-scale model of this marvel at the Smithsonian's National Air and Space Museum; it confuses you right away because the cockpit seems to be facing the tail. Then you realize that the wings are swept forward, not back, that what looks like a tail is a canard, a small lifting surface ahead of the wings.

This isn't an embarrassing engineering error, but a deliberate attempt to build a fighter plane with little drag and no stability. The more stable an aircraft, the harder it is to maneuver with speed and surprise. Forward-swept wings are utterly unstable and cut drag to the minimum, but the stresses on the wing tips are so great that only recently developed composite materials can stand them and still be light enough to fly.

In flight, the X-29 is fast as a fly, slippery as wet soap, agile as an idea. No one is told, nor seems to care, what Mach number it can hit. We now realize that simply streaking through the sky like the hammers of hell doesn't get the work done. The X-29, according to a film of a test flight, can do things that aren't in any book.

How can a man handle a beast as dicey as this? The answer is, he can't. No human can sense the forces on such a plane quickly enough to keep it flying. Three computers with back-ups check the plane's altitude and the pressures on it 40 times a

Facing Graphite-epoxy composites make the forward-swept wings of the Grumman X-29 possible; sheet metal on the forward edges would twist upwards at high speeds and cause the plane to fly out of control. Flying the highly unstable X-29 requires fly-by-wire controls at any speed—a trend that will continue in future planes.

Right The Lockheed F-117A stealth fighter remains shrouded in secrecy—usually flying at night—although it carried out strikes in Panama in December 1989 and has been operating with the 4450th Tactical Group at Nellis Air Force Base in Nevada for several years. The F-117's arrowhead shape—a new edition of the old "flying wing" concept—wouldn't stay airborne without fly-by-wire and stability augmentation systems. But pilots who have flown the F-117 unanimously reject its media nickname, "Wobbly Goblin," and speak highly of the plane's maneuverability, especially at low altitudes, below most enemy radar. Designing the F-117A for low-level precision strikes, Lockheed gave the plane a minimal radar signature by faceting its surfaces. The plane's skin is broken up into a myriad of small, flat segments which confuse enemy radar by scattering it at too many angles to form a clear pattern.

Facing There won't be an operational combat version of the X-29; it was built to explore what can be done with fly-by-wire controls and forward-swept wings. But the United States Air Force has begun testing prototypes from Lockheed and Northrop for an advanced tactical fighter to replace the F-15 at the end of the decade.

second, reacting instantly to every change, correcting every twitch, doing the work of flying.

The pilot simply tells the computer system what he wants to do. To make a left turn, he moves stick and rudder left. This sends a suggestion to the black boxes. They figure out how far they can go to obey the pilot's wish without tumbling out of the sky. If two computers disagree about what the plane can do, the third one casts the deciding vote. I like to think of them working it out:

"Sharp left? Okay, we can do that."

"No we can't! We'll pull a high-speed stall and snap roll and then spin in. We'll buy the damn farm."

And then the third computer: "Hey, cool it, you guys! We can make the turn, but maybe not quite as sharp as this hot shot wants."

And so, in the tiniest fraction of a second, the pilot's vague urge to turn left becomes reality. This is the essence of flying by wire.

Since the X-29 is on display, it's old stuff in the minds of designers, who think a generation ahead. And to fighter pilots, past and present, it once more prompts the old question: Is our species endangered?

Putting aside the easing of East-West tensions and the unlikelihood of bombing our current enemies—drug producers and terrorists—into oblivion with the help of screaming jet fighters, it surely must be true that the planes of tomorrow will not need

Above Russian fighter pilot Valery Menitsky tests new aircraft for the Mikoyan Design Bureau.

Right Pilots of the *Armée de l'Air* enjoy 360-degree visibility from the cockpits of their Mirage 2000s.

Facing Since 1969, qualified Navy fighter pilots have been attending the five-week Naval Fighter Weapons School at the Naval Air Station, Miramar, California. Informally known as "Topgun," the program was created to remedy the lack of air combat skills among F-4 pilots in Vietnam. Topgun's role today is to cultivate leaders and teachers among fighter pilots, the individuals whose example—like Mick Mannock's or Oswald Boelcke's long ago—sharpens the skills of everyone they fly with.

anything so obsolete as a human in the cockpit. Even today's F-16 jockey, trained to perfection in mind and body, experienced in reading myriad electronic messages, trussed in a pressure suit to withstand the G's of violent maneuvers, cannot hope to make correct decisions and act on them as instantly as a computer. Those black boxes can fly you to the moon, for God's sake!

Yet there are moments in any kind of flight when an illogical, instinctive, inspired input is suddenly needed—a time for controlled recklessness. So far, no computer can handle this kind of directive. It can only be hatched in the human computer—the brain. And the kind of brain with the right mixture of emotions—courage, madness, passion, and blinding revelation—has so far belonged either to a woman or to a fighter pilot.

Surely, somehow, they'll both evade extinction.

Photography Credits

B. ARPS/PHOTRI: page 55.
ED BAUMGARTEN/Tailhook Photo Service: page 151 (upper).
BETTMANN ARCHIVE: pages 81 (right), 110 (left),
127 (lower), 136 (left and right), and 192 (lower).
GERARD BEERENS: page 203.
BRITISH AEROSPACE, INC.: page 205.
V. CHEREDINTSEV/Tass/Sovphoto: page 187 (lower).
BILL CRUMP: pages 104 (lower), 111, 116-17, 126 (upper), 130,
139 (lower), and 149.
JOE CUPIDO: pages 1, 133 (upper and lower), 166, 167, 170 (upper),
174 (upper), 175 (lower), 176-77, 178 (lower), 184, 190-91, 193, 196,
199, 214, 216, 217 (upper), 219, and 226 (left).
GLENN H. CURTISS MUSEUM OF LOCAL HISTORY: page 88.
DAVID DOUBILET: pages 84-85, 97, 98-99, 106, 113 (lower), and
137 (upper).
BARRY DOWSETT: pages 37, 42, 46, and 101.
DICK DURRANCE II: pages 18-19.
ALAIN ERNOULT: pages 2, 4, 6, 8-9, 20, 22 (left), 23, 24 (lower),
27, 29, 45, 48, 61, 62-63, 86 (lower), 87 (upper and lower), 102, 104
(upper), 107, 108, 109 (right), 112, 113 (upper), 120-21, 121,
132 (upper), 137 (lower), 151 (lower), 206 (upper), 207, 220-21, and
226 (right).
ERNOULT/International Defense Images: front cover and page 228.
WILLIAM B. FOLSOM/Arms Communications: page 218.
KENNETH GARRETT: pages 122-23 and 141.
ROBERT GENAT/Arms Communications: pages 212-13.
JAMES GILBERT COLLECTION: pages 117 (upper) and 119 (upper
and lower).
GARY GLADSTONE: page 58.
GRANGER COLLECTION: pages 32 (left) and 72.
JOSEPH A. GRYSON/Tailhook Photo Service: page 173 (upper).
GRUMMAN CORPORATION: pages 222 and 225.
KEN HACKMAN/U.S. Air Force/Arms Communications: page 182.
KIRBY HARRISON/Blue Yonder Photo: page 100.
ERICH HARTMANN COLLECTION: pages 114 (lower) and 115.
DAVID HATHCOX/Arms Communications: page 227.
C. J. HEATLEY III: pages 194-95 and 198.
THE HOOK: page 188.
RANDY JOLLY/Arms Communications: page 197.
HERMAN J. KOKOJAN/Black Star: pages 17, 180, and 217 (lower).
KOKU-FAN/Arms Communications: page 204 (upper).
TIM LAMING: pages 165, 178 (upper), 179, 206 (lower), and 211.
ALAN LANDAU/Blue Thunder Pictures: pages 204 (lower) and 210
(lower).
MARSHALL LEFAVOR/U.S. Navy/Blue Thunder Pictures: pages 200-201.
HOWARD LEVY: pages 25, 30, 32 (right), 34, 38, 40, 51, 54, 57, 64, 67,
80, 83, 89, 91, 92 (lower), 95, 105 (upper and lower), 139 (upper), 154,
and 163.
B. J. LONG COLLECTION/Convair: page 173 (lower).
CARLOS LORCH: page 210 (upper).
MacGILLIVRAY FREEMAN FILMS/Du Pont: page 3.
LARRY MILBERRY: pages 158 (lower), 160, and 161.
MILITARY HISTORY INSTITUTE: page 59.
NIGEL MOLL: pages 86 (upper), 142, 150, 152-53, and 175 (upper).

ROBERT P. MORRISON/FPG International: page 15.
RUSSELL MUNSON: pages 10, 122, 124-25, and 129.
NATIONAL AIR AND SPACE MUSEUM, Smithsonian Institution: pages 21, 22
(right), 24 (upper), 26, 31, 33, 39, 41 (upper), 43, 44, 50, 53, 56, 65,
66 (upper and lower), 68, 75, 76, 82, 92 (upper), 93 (upper and lower),
94 (upper), 96, 103 (upper and lower), 109 (left), 110 (right), 114
(upper), 117 (lower), 118 (upper and lower), 125, 126 (lower), 128 (left
and right), 131, 140, 143, 146, 157 (upper), 158 (upper), 171 (right),
174 (lower), and 189 (upper).
NATIONAL ARCHIVES: pages 12, 13, 16, 35, 69, 127 (upper), 132 (lower),
134, 135 (upper and lower), 138, and 157 (lower).
SGT. DAVID S. NOLAN: page 202.
NOVOSTI/Sovphoto: pages 189 (lower) and 209.
PHOTRI: pages 81 (left), 94 (lower), 147, 156, 181, 185 (lower), and
200.

DAVID ROLAND: pages 73, 74, and 78-79.
A. J. SHORTT/National Aviation Museum (Canada): page 162.
V. SHUSTOV/Novosti/Sovphoto: page 187 (upper).
ERIK SIMONSEN: pages 145, 208, and 215.
JAMES SUGAR/Black Star: pages 168-69, and 169.
TAILHOOK PHOTO SERVICE: pages 90, 172, and 186.
TASS/Sovphoto: page 185 (upper).
JIM THOMPSON: pages 41 (lower) and 47.
CLAUDIO TOSELLI/Delta: page 171 (left).
BEN ULLINGS/Delta: page 164.
U.S. AIR FORCE: page 224.
U.S. AIR FORCE MUSEUM: pages 52, 71, 159, 170 (lower), 183, and
192 (upper).
U.S. NAVY: page 77.

Acknowledgments

Every writer who tackles the story of aviation must fall back on the previous work of other writers. I have done so unabashedly, and I thank them all, the long-gone chroniclers of World War I, the live-and-kicking authorities on latter-day flying like Mike Spick, C.J. "Heater" Heatley, Dewitt Copp, my old Smithsonian friends, Walter Boyne, Don Lopez, and especially Dick Hallion, this book's designated technical expert. I've read their works faithfully. I've also gone over another sometimes useful source—my old logbook.

Edwards Park

The publisher would also like to give special thanks to Guy Aceto, *Air Force* magazine; Nick Apple, Air Force Museum; Melissa Keiser and the staff of the National Air and Space Museum; and Virginia Torres of the Confederate Air Force for their help in gathering the photographs for this book.